Growing Love in Christian Marriage

Third Edition / Couple's Manual

RICHARD and JOAN HUNT

Abingdon Press / Nashville

GROWING LOVE IN CHRISTIAN MARRIAGE
Couple's Manual / Third Edition
Copyright © 2013 by Abingdon Press

Verses marked (TLB) are taken from The Living Bible, © 1971. Used by permission of Tyndale House Publishers, Inc., Wheaton,
IL 60189. All rights reserved.

Verses marked NRSV are from the New Revised Standard Version of the Bible, © 1989, by the Division of Christian Education of
the National Council of the Churches of Christ in the United States of America.

Scripture quotations noted RSV are from the Revised Standard Version of the Bible, © 1946, 1952, 1971, by the Division of Chris-
tian Education of the National Council of Churches of Christ in the USA. Used by permission.
Scripture quotations noted JBP are from The New Testament in Modern English, by J. B. Phillips. Copyright © 1972 by Collins
Publ., London, England.

This book is printed on acid-free, elemental chlorine-free paper.

ISBN 978-1-4267-5790-7

18 19 20—15 14 13 12
MANUFACTURED IN THE UNITED STATES OF AMERICA

CONTENTS

PERSPECTIVES ON MARRIAGE

I love you. And, I love you, too.
Marriage is about love and also about faith, hope, power, and much more. First Corinthians 13 describes love, grounded in faith and hope, and expressed through the power of action. These themes are probably familiar to you. As you read this Bible chapter together, note how power is expressed in your communication and behaviors that express love, such as being patient, kind, not irritable or demanding. These actions and communications are your power to love.

As a basic operator's manual for marriage, this couples book follows four interrelated themes: faith, hope, love, and power. Like the facets of a finely cut diamond, your focus on each theme is always in the context of the other three as background. Faith expressed in covenant commitment is the foundation for your relationship. Hope energizes and renews your lifelong journey together. Love expressed in caring relationships as a couple and with your families, work, and the world plays a major role in your marriage. Power is revealed through your actions, communications, resources, and behaviors.

Wife: If I had the gift of being able to speak in other languages,

Husband: And could speak in every language there is in all of heaven and earth,

Wife: But didn't love others,

Husband: I would only be making noise.

Wife: If I had the gift of prophecy and knew all about what is going to happen in the future,

Husband: But didn't love others,

Wife: What good would it do?

Husband: Even if I had the gift of faith so that I could speak to a mountain and make it move,

Wife: I would still be nothing without love.

Husband: Love is very patient and kind.

Wife: Love is never boastful or proud.

Husband: Love is never haughty or selfish or rude.

Wife: Love does not demand its own way.

Husband: Love is not irritable or touchy.

Wife: Love does not hold grudges and will hardly even notice when others do it wrong.

Husband: Love rejoices whenever truth wins out.

Wife: If you love someone, you will be loyal to that person, no matter what the cost.

Husband: You will always believe in that person,

Wife: Always expect the best of that person,

Husband: Always stand your ground in supporting that person.

Wife: There are three gifts that remain:

Both: Faith, hope, and love—but the greatest of these is love.

By Couples for You as a Couple

Marriage preparation begins when you decide to marry and continues through at least your first two years of marriage. Your life experiences influence your current relationship, but most important are the patterns of relating you use now.

We, the couples who developed this guide, have experienced much joy and happiness in our marriages. At times, of course, we have found our marriages difficult or frustrating, a normal experience in any healthy relationship. Our marriages change as we develop as caring persons and spouses. By working through difficulties, we have grown as individuals and in appreciation of our respective spouses. Positive patterns, such as expressing appreciation and having fun together, keep us happily together. Marriage truly is "for better, for worse, for richer, for poorer, in sickness and in health."

Your Marriage Is Unique

Each marriage is different from the others, yet we all affirm basic values and skills that we describe in these pages. Examine them carefully to see how they fit your situation. You may reject some suggestions, and we accept your decisions as signs of your growth. You may discover additional insights from other sources, and we encourage you in exploring those insights on the basis of your commitment to God and to each other.

In this guide we raise many issues and questions for you to explore together, but we cannot give all the answers. Part of your joy comes from the exciting opportunity to create your own answers and to make your relationship all that you want it to be.

It does not matter what other couples do or do not do in their marriages. What does matter is that you and your partner live your lives in ways that are most satisfying to you, as you understand yourselves in relation to God and others.

Resource Persons for You

Your church is deeply interested in you, your marriage, and your family. Be sure to have an open line of communication with your pastor, minister, or counselor. Through them and the church you have access to support for your marriage. Every couple needs friends and relatives who encourage and support them in their lifelong marriage journey. Their com-ments are worth serious consideration, whether you agree with them or not. If your church has a trained mentor or Caring Couples ministry, seek them out to support healthy marriages at every stage of life.

Some communities have a "community marriage policy" in which all clergy agree to require couples to complete a marriage preparation program before they marry.

Whether you are engaged, just married, or married many years, comparing others' views offers valuable ways to see yourselves and your relationship so you are free to choose options, learn about yourselves and each other, and compare your goals and experiences with those of others.

Private Couple Times

Talking together privately is essential to keep your relationship going. Your private discussions and practices as a couple are your most important dimension of marriage preparation and enrichment. The suggested "Explore" exercises and questions to consider are intended to encourage you to find your common vision for your marriage and commit yourselves to grow as a couple. Through these pages, we invite you into an intimate sharing with your partner. Exploring your relationship can be fun, although at times it may be upsetting. Sharing your dreams, hopes, and deepest feelings and thoughts with your partner strengthens your relationship and helps you choose the direction you want it to take.

Since this guide is addressed to all couples in many different circumstances, select the sections and topics that fit your situation. You may read together or separately, coming together to talk about your findings. Use whatever order and style that works for you. The important thing is to explore all the topics that are relevant to you.

For some subjects you may have easy and ready answers. For others, you may need to pause and dig deeper to find suitable agreements and compromises. Most couples have some issues with which they may struggle for years before learning to cope well in those areas.

In this process with your partner, you can become more confident with your decisions regarding your relationship as you continue to explore its many facets. Sometimes sincere disagreement and confrontation may be especially helpful as you examine your expectations, improve your communication skills, and establish new goals together.

The quality of your private time is the most important factor in maintaining hope and joy in your marriage. Although you may be caught up in a myriad of wedding details, we hope that you and your partner will schedule enough private time together to work through much of the material in this book. Sharing hopes, dreams, goals, and expectations will help you grow as a couple.

Deciding About Marriage

Although the suggestions and exercises in this guide seem to presume that you and your partner will marry each other, we assume only that you want to explore your relationship in greater depth, so that you can make your own decisions about marriage. We want you and your partner to be independent of others so you can freely enter into marriage if you so choose. Be honest with yourselves. Decisions about your relationship are yours to make and live out.

In your explorations you may discover insights about yourselves and your relationship that will lead you to decide not to marry. Perhaps every couple experiences some doubts about marriage, but persistent or serious reservations are important to consider. If you discover that you really do not want to marry each other, it is more loving to exit before the wedding rather than later. Your decision not to marry now, although painful, will be less hurtful than a separation or divorce later.

Conflicts provide opportunities for growth. Even very happy couples will have periods of difficulty, disagreement, discouragement, uncertainty, and pain. If you both deal honestly and constructively with those differences, you can grow in new or unexpected ways. If some conflicts seem too difficult to handle, talk with your minister, a support couple, or a counselor about finding help.

Other Couples for Support

Talking with other couples provides several benefits:

Friendship: Find encouragement as you establish yourselves as a married couple.

Information: Find additional readings, workshops, and marriage enrichment opportunities for refreshment, reminder, and renewal.

Examples: Other couples show how they are living their marriage, thus adding to the models of marriage from which you can choose for yourselves.

Accountability: With your permission, couples can assist you to do exercises and discuss important issues. If your explorations trigger unexpected anger, fear, or uncertainty, a minister or counselor may help you regain perspective so you can grow.

Feedback: Some couples can observe your interactions and give you feedback and coaching for change.

In addition to meetings with you, your pastor and supporting couples may offer premarital preparation through couples groups. Check with your pastor about these possibilities.

Postwedding: Your First Two Years— Continuing Your Honeymoon

A wedding is for a day, but a marriage is for a lifetime.

During the first two years after your wedding, you are establishing your patterns as spouses and as a couple. Some 50 percent of all divorces occur during these first years when spouses are making the transition to being a couple, which often brings stresses and conflicts. Success comes from finding cooperative patterns for coping with the little adjustments, as well as the big ones.

Marriage involves communities of persons who cooperate and support one another in times of joy and trouble. Just as you encourage others, so others want to support you as you shape your lives and marriage. You already know some of these persons in your families, among your friends, and in your church.

Couples groups and classes provide opportunities to meet other couples, exchange information about marriage dynamics, and share mutual support at each stage of marriage. Marriage Enrichment events invite couples to join together to strengthen their marriage relationships.

Churches may join together to offer a GROWING LOVE IN CHRISTIAN MARRIAGE couples' group or class to expand on topics in each of the four themes in this guide. The format for the group may be one evening a week across five to ten weeks, two or three one-day sessions, or three to five half-day sessions, scheduled over several months during the year.

By talking with successfully married couples you can observe patterns you would like to have in your own marriage. In most churches there are couples who would enjoy having you talk with them about their marriage. We encourage you and your partner to seek them out.

Sometime during the first months after your wedding, plan at least one visit with your sponsoring couple or your minister. You might invite them to your home or meet at another convenient place. Your minister may have information about these opportunities, and you can consult resources listed in this book.

If you move from your present church, we encourage you to reestablish a relationship with a local church in your new community where you can meet other couples with similar values, goals, and concerns.

Previous Relationships

Whether this is your first marriage, or another marriage, or you have been married many years, your experiences (both good and bad) in your previous romantic relationships are part of what you bring to your current marriage. Where you have been or what happened in the past is important, yet what matters most is what you have learned from your previous experiences.

If you are divorced, you may still have feelings of pain, anger, relief, remorse, rejection, or uncertainty that you and your current partner need to address. If you are living with your partner now or lived with another partner in the past, talk about how your marriage will be similar or different. If your previous marriage was ended by the death of your spouse, acknowledge feelings such as sadness or loneliness. If you already have children, talk about the complications of joining in a new family. (See Explore Guides in Section 3.4.)

Start with where you are now. Celebrate the good feelings and habits you bring to each other. Find ways to grow through the challenges you still face in yourself and with each other. This basic book addresses many topics in the themes of faith, hope, love, and power that still apply to any marriage, whether your first or a subsequent marriage.

Use the Explore guides to discuss together all the issues and topics that are important to you. Then go to additional references for specifics that may not be fully described here. Talk with your pastor and mentor couples about any concerns you have. In the white spaces and margins of this guide, add your notes, comments, and references.

EXPLORE A: Plan Your Growth

Take some time now as a couple to talk about the process of exploration described in this section. Look over the topics in each of the following chapters to get a general idea of the direction your own discussions might take. Share your thoughts about these possibilities with your partner.

1. How do you feel about looking openly at your relationship? Sometimes open, candid exploration may feel risky or uncomfortable. We think you can cope with these risky or difficult areas.

2. Some say the five most feared words in marriage are, "Let's talk about our relationship." What do you think?

3. Which topics seem easier to discuss? Which do you want to explore first? Begin with those chapters and use them in a order. Return later to the others.

4. It may help to have a notebook in which you can write down thoughts, feelings, comments, and wishes that occur to each of you as you explore your relationship. You also might save stories, pictures, cartoons, poems, or sayings that are especially meaningful and share these with each other.

5. Share your reactions about different types of marriages that you know, such as couples you know or who are portrayed on television or in movies.

Marriage as Covenant

From many experiences in family, media, previous relationships, and other sources you bring assumptions to marriage that you are continually exploring and modifying. We invite you together to describe your own meanings, expectations, wants, needs, and gifts for your marriage.

What makes a marriage Christian is the covenant of each spouse to love the other one, based on his or her commitment to God as known in Jesus Christ. Marriage as a covenant between spouses is Christ-centered in this promise of love and grace and is supremely expressed in the appearance of Jesus as the Christ, the Messiah-God present in the world.

Christians hold marriage to be a sacred covenant relationship more than merely a legal institution. Christian faith is the foundation for your home. Your marriage is a dynamic, growing system of interactions between God, spouses, and family members. These spiritual formation patterns shape your household, the ways you love and cherish each other, and relate to family, work, and world.

Freedom Comes From
God's Covenant Grace

Deep in every person is a hunger to be unique and to be accepted just as he or she is, without any strings attached. To be loved unconditionally, just as I am, frees me to drop my defenses, to grow, and to love others.

Christians may differ concerning some details of marriage, yet most hold that marriage involves both genders with equally shared power. Marriage means one woman and one man with both persons having equal opportunity to talk, to listen, and to share love and power.

Christians enter marriage in response to God's love. Choosing to marry involves each person's fundamental decisions about whether to be married and about self, gender, and control. God cares for us all, just as we are, whether single, married, widowed, or divorced. Every person, however, married or not, makes this decision.

Jesus used the wedding feast to suggest the excitement and joy between humanity and God. Marriage is a relationship through which we learn more about love. It is a parable of God's relationship to the world. The continuing concern of spouses for each other can become an example of this trust (". . . Do

not let anyone be faithless to the wife of his youth. For I hate divorce, says the LORD of hosts" (Malachi 2:15-16, NRSV).

Each event calls for caring and loving relationships; many passages in the New Testament describe this "more excellent way of love." The discussions of marriage in Ephesians 5:21-33 and in Colossians 3:18-21 give examples of unconditional love in marriage and family relationships. Compared to life in ancient times, this model of marriage was a big step forward.

Commitment Gives Freedom

Your sincere commitment to each other frees you to evaluate past ways of doing things, so that you can improve yourselves and your marriage. It allows you to be yourselves, to withdraw occasionally from each other for personal renewal and insight and be open and honest without destroying your relationship.

Because of your commitment, you both can continue to develop and grow throughout your lives. Your basic unconditional pledge is the foundation of your willingness to work out whatever difficulties you may encounter. Such grace in marriage really is amazing. In these ways marriage is a major channel for spiritual growth and formation.

Marriage is not an end in itself, but one means toward a goal: the development of the persons involved. Through marriage a more complete quality of living can be achieved. Based on the love that you find with each other, you can look beyond your marriage and reach out to others in the world.

Communion: Marriage Is Like
a Sacrament

Christian sacraments are events that express God's acceptance of persons into new relationships in the Christian community. Although most Protestant Christians consider baptism, "naming in Christ," and the Lord's Supper, "communion with Christ," as the only official sacraments, marriage can have the sacramental quality of being a means to God's grace to grow in love.

This special relationship of communion happens when partners fully accept each other into the special "one woman-one man" community of Christian marriage. Others also benefit from seeing the quality of mutual affirmation that your marriage relationship demonstrates.

The key concept in these understandings of Christian marriage is God's continuing unquestioning grace-filled love and the couple's sharing of this love with each other and with others. This covenant model includes at least two basic elements. The first element is your mutual intention as partners to love and to cherish each other, as God has loved you. This is your basic goal. From this comes the second: your mutual commitment to work, through your relationship in love, for your own growth, for the growth of your spouse, and then together for the growth of others.

Many Ways You Can Grow

We experience joyful hope in marriage because our Christian faith centers on love and willingness to forgive each other—two essentials that rise above the mores of every generation. The standard for measuring the quality of every marriage is love, forgiveness, and renewal. This gives hope. You express these in your own unique ways, yet successful couples agree that hope for the future of every marriage depends upon both spouses being able and willing to care deeply for each other. Forgiveness is part of love because it resets the relationship in ways that allow the couple to try again.

You renew your marriage as you grow in love across your lifetime journey together. You can continue your growth through couples retreats, classes, celebrations, anniversaries, and regular marriage check-ups. Reaching out to support other couples helps you and your spouse to appreciate each other and renew your own joy in your marriage.

Growing in love means change. You may fear being displaced or excluded more than change itself. As you nurture each other, you learn new patterns for making your marriage strong and healthy, which encourages you to share your successes with others.

You Can Do It—Your Journey Has Already Begun

We hope you laugh together, talk a lot, and hug each other often as you venture into the many facets of your relationship. You may cry at times or become angry, yet these reactions also express how important you are to each other.

If this self-discovery process is new to you, go slower and feel your way into some of these areas. You may be pleasantly surprised by how often you agree and are able to reach out and affirm each other. Some couples want someone to tell them exactly what to think and do in marriage, but we believe that God invites couples to discover for themselves the many great truths that marriage offers.

Our Continuing Blessing to You

Continue to seek God's guidance in your process of growth as individuals and as a couple. Agree on the ways you will use this guide. May you love and cherish each other increasingly throughout your lives.

EXPLORE B: Meanings of Marriage

Discuss your ideas about marriage in relation to what you have read. One possibility is for each partner to share feelings and then to talk about its meaning for you as a couple.

Independently, write some words or phrases that express what your marriage means to you; then compare notes. You may describe a movie or drama about a couple and identify specific positive and/or negative views of marriage expressed. You might also locate pictures, cartoons, music lyrics, poems, or other materials that help you talk about your marriage and its meanings for you and for others.

How do you feel about examining your relationship? As a couple, what are your reactions if . . .
    you both do not want to enter this process?
    you want this process, but your partner does not?
    your partner wants this process, but you do not?
    you both are eager to begin?

Considering your relationship in marriage (whether pre- or postwedding) involves much more than merely reading a book. You need time to talk with each other about what you want and expect your relationship. Use the Explore exercises often.

Our Engagement Covenant

Engagement is a special time in your life. It is your opportunity to examine yourselves as a potential married couple and to maximize your chance to have a lifelong committed relationship. Building a relationship based on values, commitment, and faith takes time, effort, and discipline.

Premarital sexual activities, living together, combined finances, and/or other arrangements give a couple a false sense of commitment that makes it more difficult to be open and honest with each other during the engagement period. Sex can become a poor substitute for mature communication and meaningful exploration that enhance growth.

We invite you to make your engagement time extra special by postponing sexual intimacy in order to concentrate your full energy and attention to strengthening your relationship.

Research shows that couples who marry after having lived together or who had premarital sexual intimacies are more likely to divorce. This may be because they have not fully committed to each other with deep mutual respect. This makes it easy to exit marriage later when unexamined issues arise.

Draw a circle to represent your marriage including both partners and Christ at the center giving you guidance, understanding, patience, and love throughout your lives both individually and in your marriage together. Just as primary teeth hold the spacing for permanent teeth as we mature, so may this engagement covenant be a bridge to your faithful Christian marriage covenant.

Your pastor can offer an engagement liturgy and additional helps to supplement this basic agreement you make about your engagement. Among helpful biblical references are 1 Corinthians 7 and 1 Thessalonians 4.

(Adapted from Forrest Burdette United Methodist Church Caring Couples Ministry.)

Engagement Covenant

Relying on God's grace I value myself and I value you. I ask God to be present with us as we engage to carefully explore whether to enter marriage together. With care and honesty we agree to examine in depth ourselves and our possible future together, always speaking the truth in love.

I invite God to be in all aspects of our discussions about our lives, including physical, emotional, social, and spiritual. We are not alone. When we include prayer to help guide us throughout life, it helps give a Christian perspective to our lives in marriage and as individuals.

During our engagement as problems occur, I want to be more patient and understanding through love. I invite help from our pastor and support couple, as well as seeking God's guidance through prayer. This pattern opens support to strengthen our marriage.

I will lay aside anything that may bias me or predispose me either to marry or not to marry. Among these possible pressures are living arrangements, sexual activities, financial considerations, and expectations from families and friends.

I pledge to commit our engagement time to these purposes.

_____   _____
Woman   *Man*

THEME ONE

FAITH AS COVENANTAL COMMITMENT

GRACE FOR YOUR COEQUAL COVENANT

We know that all things work together for good for those who love God, who are called according to his purpose. . . . For I am convinced that neither death, nor life, nor angels, nor rulers, nor things present, nor things to come, nor powers, nor height, nor depth, nor anything else in all creation, will be able to separate us from the love of God in Christ Jesus our Lord.   *(Romans 8:28, 38-39, NRSV)*

The fruit of the Spirit is love, joy, peace, patience, kindness, goodness, faithfulness, gentleness, and self-control.   *(Galatians 5:22-23, NRSV)*

To Timothy. . . I am reminded of your sincere faith . . . that lived first in your grandmother Lois and your mother Eunice and now, I am sure, lives in you.   *(2 Timothy 1:2, 5, NRSV)*

MAN TO THE WOMAN:

In the name of God,
I, Name, take you, Name, to be my wife,
to have and to hold from this day forward,
for better, for worse, for richer, for poorer,
in sickness and in health, to love and to cherish,
until we are parted by death.
This is my solemn vow.

WOMAN TO THE MAN:

In the name of God,
I, Name, take you, Name, to be my husband,
to have and to hold from this day forward,
for better, for worse, for richer, for poorer,
in sickness and in health, to love and to cherish,
until we are parted by death.
This is my solemn vow.

(From "The Service of Christian Marriage" in The United Methodist Hymnal, *page 867.)*

EXPLORE 1: Meaning of Covenant Faith Commitment

Here are some possible meanings of covenant faith or faith covenant. Add others that you think are important. Then select the words that you think most express what faith, covenant, and commitment mean for you. Talk together about your meanings.

vow	pledge	troth	promise
trust	contract	assurance	stability
unconditional	long-term	bond	dependable
commitment	be there	grace	decision
perspective	confidence	worldview	gift
determination	virtue	values	will

1.1

FOUNDATIONS: I, YOU, and WE

To understand your partner. . . begin by understanding yourself. Creating a successful marriage is more a matter of being the right partner than of finding the right partner.

On Faith, Commitment, and Covenant

The theme of faith as covenant commitment invites you to examine what you bring to your marriage in the context of the foundational life meanings you hold for yourselves.

Your marriage covenant comes out of your faith and your ways of seeing yourselves, the world, and God. Covenant is your decision to commit yourselves to each other, unconditionally and without qualification of any kind. Covenant means you stay with your vow to love and care for your spouse, regardless of what others do.

Your faith is the basis for your worldview, your character, your life priorities, and your attitudes toward commitment, vows, marriage, and life. Faith points to what you trust. Based on your "I/Thou" relationship of faith you can rephrase questions such as "Who am I?" and "Who are we?" to affirmation statements such as "I am/ We are" and "I am not/We are not." As in a covenant your promises become as solid as a rock.

You bring to your marriage all of your heritage from your past. This includes your home and family experiences as a growing child and adolescent, the results of your previous romantic relationships, attitudes formed from participating in many types of groups, and images imposed on you from the mass media. While these events shape your self and worldview, they do not determine how you will live your own marriage.

Identity and Faith

Like talking and walking, all the components of faithful covenant are lifelong elements. The impor-

tance you give to keeping promises, acting with integrity, being dependable, and other matters of virtue and character greatly affect how you will daily live your marriage vows. These are the values and virtues that you use to define who you are, your identity, the real you.

Through covenant, you commit to virtues that are commendable qualities, traits, and merits, the positive virtues you want as your standards for right living in your marriage, home, and lives. In this way marriage becomes a major channel for your spiritual formation throughout life.

Covenant says you are happily married because you want to, not because you are required to stay together. This is the big difference between external constraint and internal dedication, which finds renewed joy in new ways of being together.

Dedication to covenant together is a lifestyle, your "marital status." Covenant is your long-term commitment that provides dependability and security for growing in love throughout your lifelong journey together. It is your fundamental, unconditional determination to make your marriage work. In your journey you deepen your promise as it is tested through life's events.

Who we were yesterday may affect us but does not control who we are today. All your life experiences have influenced your current relationship. Although the focus of this book is on the first years of marriage, you can adapt every topic to your current stage and circumstances.

Unique Individuals

You are a complex, unique individual—a special person. Your identity is the sum total of all your behaviors, habits, attitudes, priorities, virtues, and goals. You may think of character as "who you are" and personality as "how you act" or the characteristics that enable you and others to identify you as you.

As adults, we ask, "Who am I?" and we then shape it into the affirmation, "I am . . . a certain way"—a unique person. We invite you to look at some major areas of your individualities: your physical appearance, your families of origin, your attitudes and thought patterns, your habits and behaviors, and how you use your power to love or to hurt.

Look at yourselves, your backgrounds, your personal characteristics, and the beliefs and goals that you each bring to your relationship.

Understanding and affirming oneself, whether single or married, is essential to wholesome living. God has created you and given you the freedom and power, within limits, to control and shape your world and your life as you choose. Everything we do has consequences. Creative growth is a lifetime process, and God sustains you in every circumstance. This is God's freely given grace.

Being and Living

Your own personal faith or spirituality is at the core of your being. On the basis of your faith each of you defines yourself as being who you are and are not, as "I am" and its contrast, "I am not." Although it may seem strange today, one of the early names for God is "I Am" (Exodus 3:14).

Your entire personhood, character, and all that you are and have expresses your faith, your fundamental assumptions about life, your belief—or what you live by. Faith traditions talk about this as "core being" or "soul." Your identity, innermost being, your "I am" is beyond words and language, yet is constantly expressed through your words and behaviors. The real you, your complete self, character, ego, identity, or body-mind-soul-spirit, is the way you respond to God's creative calling to you to be a person in the twenty-first century.

The good news of the Christian faith is that God loves us just as we are. God has made a covenant (Jeremiah 31:33-34; John 3:16) with us to love us unconditionally. God's covenant expresses the guarantee that God loves us all the time, even at times when we feel most unlovable. This is our model for loving each other unconditionally in marriage as God has loved us as we are. Growing in love is your lifetime vocation or calling, continually expressed in all that you do in marriage, family, career, and world relationships.

Attitudes and Perspectives

Attitudes are your perspectives on life—the way you look at others and at the world, including what you expect from yourself and from others. These views include the way you are likely to act toward

---

EXPLORE 1.1A: "I am . . ." "I am not . . ." "We are . . ." "We are not . . ."

How do you each complete the statement, "I am . . ."? Try saying this phrase aloud several times to your partner. Each time, use a different word or phrase to describe the way you see yourself. Here are some possibilities:

I am . . . a woman/man . . . successful . . . funny . . . attractive . . . honest . . . smart

The parallel phrase, "I am not," describes how you are different from others and sets the boundaries for who you are. Try completing this phrase, such as:

I am not . . . lazy . . . stupid . . . an alien . . . expressive . . . a loner

After exchanging "I am" and "I am not" statements, share your feelings about describing yourself, as:

When I talk about myself, I feel . . .
When you describe yourself to me, I feel . . .

Then try the same exercise using stem statements, "We are . . ." and "We are not . . ." to define yourselves as a couple, combining your strengths as a woman and a man who choose to stay married to each other.

your partner and toward others, and the way you interpret events.

When you say that a person is confident or active, you are expressing your view of that person's behaviors. Since your views about others shape your feelings and actions toward them, one way to grow is to look carefully at the way you view yourself and your partner.

Attitudes and Ways of Thinking

Physical Appearance and Genetic Givens

Your physical appearance is a combination of your genetic inheritance, your skills for caring for your body, and your attitudes about yourself. Physical characteristics, like height and body proportions, are easily seen by others. Intellectual and emotional characteristics may be seen only through activities. Your experiences influence your attitudes about yourself and your ethnic identities. Genetic factors both set limits and offer opportunities in many subtle ways, such as musical or sports talent, strength, energy level, intellectual ability, emotional make-up, sensitivities, and cycles of activity and rest.

In some ways, your physical appearance is a snapshot of the visible you. Unfortunately, too often we interpret our worth or value in terms of how physically attractive we think we are to others. The way you dress, care for yourself, and use your body also are expressions of the way you feel about yourself.

Commercial advertising, television, beauty contests, and glamour magazines present a limited image of the qualities that constitute physical attractiveness. This image usually is presented as sexual attractiveness, with the implication that if we look like the idealized picture, we will be desired, accepted, and happy.

Our bodies are God's temples (1 Corinthians 3:16). Through our bodies—our physical and sexual selves—we express our attitudes of love (Romans 12; 1 Corinthians 13). As important as physical and sexual attractiveness are, it is only one of the many rich facets of ourselves that we bring to marriage.

EXPLORE 1.1B: Appearance

Your appearance expresses your unique inner beauty, which comes from the quality of honestly being yourself. Take some time to talk with your partner about physical appearance. As you think about your face and body, what evaluations do you make of yourself? Do you like your face? Do you really enjoy your body? Do you think you are too thin, too fat, or just right? Why? What do you value in your own appearance? your partner's appearance?

How much has (or did) attractiveness influence your meeting? How do your facial features and posture express your inner attitudes and feelings? Give some illustrations.

Look at some pictures of men and women of various ages. What do you like or dislike about each picture? In what ways are you similar to or different from them? How do you feel about these comparisons?

What physical challenges or chronic health conditions do you have? How are you coping with these? What limits does your body place on you? What would you like to change?

How are your ethnic identity and appearance related?

How comfortable are you with your sexual and other pleasurable body feelings? If possible, stand or sit before a mirror and ask yourself some of these questions as you view your body.

EXPLORE 1.1C: Personal Views

Listed below are several dimensions of attitudes and personality that can be used to compare your views with your partner's views. Answer independently. Be honest in answering, since this openness can help you both to grow.

Place a mark on each line to indicate the point at which you see yourself and another mark for the point at which you see your partner on each dimension. To aid your comparisons later, use this code:

F = Female's view of self
H = Female's view of man (husband)
M = Male's view of self
W = Male's view of woman (wife)

sometimes insecure :___:___:___:___:___:___:	very confident
likes to control :___:___:___:___:___:___:	likes to be controlled
very warm and caring :___:___:___:___:___:___:	cool, distant
pessimistic, sad :___:___:___:___:___:___:	happy, optimistic
active :___:___:___:___:___:___:	quiet
gives in, passive :___:___:___:___:___:___:	demanding, aggressive
tense :___:___:___:___:___:___:	relaxed
open, flexible :___:___:___:___:___:___:	closed, unbending
likes being with others :___:___:___:___:___:___:	likes being alone
likes to listen :___:___:___:___:___:___:	likes to talk
withholds affection :___:___:___:___:___:___:	always very affectionate

If you answer on two sheets, transfer those responses to this sheet with a different color pen or pencil.

As you and your partner compare your views, try to give specific instances of the attitude or characteristic. How do you feel as you discuss these areas? If you find that you feel defensive or angry, talk about these reactions. What do you do when you feel displeased about a comment from your partner? Be open to your partner's comments, and thank your partner for sharing them.

You also may talk about these attitudes and personal qualities in relation to qualities that you value, such as courage, honesty, compassion, love, and openness.

1.2

FAMILIES, RELATIVES, FRIENDS

Rediscovering Your Backgrounds

All of your life experiences, both positive and negative, contribute to the ways you live out your commitment in your marriage, family, and life. You are what you are today because of the experiences you had in previous years. Each past year is important, but the most important time is now. In a sense, your entire past has prepared you, for better or worse, for your relationship with your partner.

You are not trapped by your family experiences. You can change yourself. You can acknowledge the good skills and experiences that others have given you and resolve to improve those areas with which you are dissatisfied.

The way you remember your past is very important for you and your partner now. We encourage you to set aside a quiet evening to share some im-

portant memories in your lives. Many couples have found this personal sharing to be thought-provoking, emotionally helpful, and mutually supportive. With your partner, take time to tell some stories, listen, laugh, and perhaps cry, with a deeper appreciation of the separate experiences that each of you bring to your relationship.

You can view your childhood and adolescence as a continuing drama involving your family members and early friends as the cast of characters. You have influenced those persons, and they have influenced you. Some may be closer than relatives are to you. In addition, church and community groups are major sources of friendships.

Your sense of worth and self-confidence developed from experiences in which you felt accepted,

---

EXPLORE 1.2A: Personal Experiences

Allow plenty of time—at least an hour—for this exercise. Select some specific experiences from the list below. Then take turns describing an event in the category selected. Go through as many types of events as you can. Add other categories if you wish.

- your favorite food: as a child, as an adolescent, and now
- a movie or play that you enjoyed
- a very happy occasion
- a time you succeeded
- your favorite Bible verses or church experiences
- an age you most enjoyed
- a very funny experience

- a dream you have had many times
- a secret wish, hope, or ambition
- when you were most angry or upset
- a major sadness, disappointment, or hurt
- a fear you have never told anyone
- the biggest surprise you ever had
- a time you felt especially loved, wanted, and accepted

As you share these memories with your partner, how do you feel? How does your partner feel and/or respond?
What discoveries have each of you made about yourselves through this special sharing?
How are these memories related to your lives now?
Affectionately touch or hug your partner to express your thanks for sharing these experiences.

---

forgiven, loved, and affirmed by others. By contrast, depression and despair arose out of experiences that made you feel inadequate, angry, controlled, rejected, or unable to meet someone's expectations.

We have found that our marriages are much more the result of what we are doing now than of what was done in the past. Although you may have intense feelings about past events, you cannot go back and change them. The past is history, and your future depends upon what you are doing right now. It is in the present that you live and build for the future.

Read the following statements aloud several times:

I cannot change my past, but I can revise the way I look at and interpret my past, and I can deal with the feelings I have about past events.

I cannot change past events, but I can revise the meanings I give to those events today.

I cannot change my family background, heritage, genetic make-up, past experiences, but I can revise the meanings I give to these factors in my life.

No matter what you bring to your marriage or what you have been, the good news is that you can choose to change yourself. By making positive changes in yourself you become different, which then invites your partner to respond positively also.

There are many more dimensions to your lives that you bring to your marriage and your future together. Talk together about the ways in which you each view these factors in your marriage:

• your ethnic origin and/or identity
• customs and celebrations in your home, neighborhood
• experiences in school, friendship groups, athletics, interest groups, community
• birth order in your family
• crises, accidents, chronic problems
• spiritual and religious concerns

EXPLORE 1.2B: Relatives and Friends—Your Genogram

Which of the following relatives are in your family of origin—parents, step-parents, sisters, brothers, cousins, grandparents, uncles, aunts, guardians, others?

Select several relatives who have been or are most significant in your life. You might draw your family tree, with these names connected by lines to show family relationships (like a genogram of your family and your spouse's family).

For each relative you include:
• Describe some unique or meaningful characteristics.
• What do you especially appreciate in this person?
• What bothers you about him or her?
• In what ways are you like that relative?

Next, name some friends who are important to you. Share some of your impressions and feelings about each one.

In which community and church groups were you active while growing up? What did you learn about yourself in those groups? Did they leave you with any positive and/or negative feelings about yourself?

Describe some experiences that have given you confidence in yourself as a worthwhile, valuable person. Which persons contributed to these experiences?

Describe some negative experiences you had. Contrast those with satisfying experiences.
• Who was involved?
• What made each experience hurtful or negative?
• How do you feel now about those experiences?

Talk with each other about important relatives, friends, and former relationships. Describe their influence on your lives today.

1.3

PERSONAL HABITS, EXPECTATIONS

Good marriages are not ready-made from heaven . . . A good marriage comes with some tools and patterns, but part of the instructions are missing, and you and your partner have to put it together yourselves . . . and sometimes the glue doesn't stick, and parts must be changed, and new resources found . . . and the joy is in the search, and the creation, and the renewal, and the journey.

"Things will be different after the wedding." "Marriage isn't what you think it is." "I'll make my partner change after we're married." "And they lived happily ever after." "Marriage takes a lot of work."

How often have you heard statements like these? Notice how each statement points to what the speaker expects or anticipates in marriage.

You each bring resources and expectations to your relationship that are important to understand and appreciate.

Expectations include the assumptions each of you makes about the things a husband and wife should do or should not do in order to have a happy marriage. These assumptions guide the way you treat each other.

As you have become better acquainted, you have formed many opinions about each other. You probably anticipate that you and your partner will act in certain ways. These predictions, based upon your hopes, dreams, and expectations, influence the way you view your relationship. You will compare what happens with what you expected to happen, and by this you will judge the happiness of your marriage.

Expectations have positive and negative aspects. Positive expectations provide a dependable structure for your relationship. Each of you usually knows what the other wants, likes, and will do in specific situations. This confidence gives both of you a sense of belonging and being fully accepted in trust and love. It also can guide the way you communicate with each other. On the other hand, when an expected response does not occur, you may feel angry, hurt, upset, confused, surprised, or afraid.

You may feel trapped by inaccurate assumptions or unrealistic expectations. Unconscious expectations may limit your love and keep you from growing as individuals and as a couple.

Being Clear and Honest About Your Expectations

A key element in your relationship is that you both continue to be clear and honest about your expectations. You need to have ways to talk about shifts in what you expect. Compare your views so you can seek new understandings and agreements about your relationship. For your marriage to continue to be satisfying, it is essential that you agree on most of your expectations. Some of your assumptions arise from experiences you had with your parents and others in your childhood family. Even if you are not aware of these expectations, they still influence you. Look at them carefully.

Some Topics for Discussion

It is important in your marriage that you each assume that you can shape your relationship in directions that you choose. Here are some areas to consider as you discuss your expectations and assumptions.

How accurate are your assumptions? Is your perception of your partner's expectations accurate? When you express your own expectations to your partner, or your partner describes his or her expectations to you, it does not mean that you agree with all these assumptions.

When do you feel caught in a triangle between your partner, others, and yourself? Although you may still appreciate your parents and others, your marriage is your primary relationship. It helps to discuss with your partner a mutual strategy to help relatives when they need you, but without allowing them to control your marriage.

How do you feel and act when events occur differently than you had anticipated? Expectations never are quite the same as reality. At those times you can learn greater patience, forgiveness, and ways to compromise, without losing integrity and individuality.

Do you anticipate that your marriage will provide everything you always wanted but seemed to lack in your life? Marriage challenges both partners to achieve desired possibilities.

You may enjoy considering some of your views. A few assumptions may be more threatening than others, or you may see only a part of some you hold.

EXPLORE 1.3A: Assumptions About Behaviors

The following statements describe some behaviors that may be assumed or expected from one or both spouses in a marriage. Use this inventory to compare some of your expectations. Answer independently before seeing your partner's answers. For each statement, indicate which person expects each behavior. Use initials or this code to show your answers:

W = usually expected of wife, although sometimes applies to husband
H = usually expected of husband, although sometimes applies to wife
O = some other arrangement, such as both partners or neither partner (After both complete, describe which arrangement you had in mind.)

Wife Thinks Husband Expects	Wife's Answer	Husband's Answer	Husband Thinks Wife Expects	
_____	_____	_____	_____	1. Likes parties and visiting with friends
_____	_____	_____	_____	2. Prefers to stay at home
_____	_____	_____	_____	3. Prepares meals
_____	_____	_____	_____	4. Cleans house; cares for pets
_____	_____	_____	_____	5. Suggests going to movies, eating out
_____	_____	_____	_____	6. Wants a night out alone sometimes
_____	_____	_____	_____	7. Gives hugs and kisses; starts lovemaking
_____	_____	_____	_____	8. Fixes things around the house or apartment
_____	_____	_____	_____	9. Decides about money
_____	_____	_____	_____	10. Takes care of children
_____	_____	_____	_____	11. Wants more affection
_____	_____	_____	_____	12. Participates in church activities
_____	_____	_____	_____	13. Compliments, encourages others
_____	_____	_____	_____	14. Chooses television programs we watch
_____	_____	_____	_____	15. _____

There are several ways you can look at your answers to this inventory. First, you can compare what you each expect with what your partner thinks you expect. Next, you can compare "wife's answers" with "husband's answers." Discuss responses to help you explore similarities and differences in your expectations.
  • Where do you try to control your partner?
  • Where do you cooperate and compromise?
  • Where are you in conflict? Why?

Where do you differ or see conflict? How do you feel about these? At which places do you misunderstand each other? Allow some time to clarify details of your assumptions. If unresolved, talk with your pastor or a counselor. At which points do you agree? How do you feel about this? Try to find the reasons for your agreement so you can strengthen your mutual expectations.

Keep examining your assumptions. Talk about the way you see yourselves and each other. Share your dreams about marriage. Try to pinpoint some of your specific actions that may contribute to the fulfillment of your expectations.

Good Habits

Habits are your personalized way of doing things. You created your habits as you responded to previous experiences and tried to find ways to deal with them. Habits influence the ways you live your commitments.

Grace means we can love each other regardless of whether we agree on a particular point, belief, or way of doing something. Even when you do not agree, being able to see your partner's point of view is an expression of grace.

You each have routines for getting up, dressing, eating, and going about your daily activities. You have speech, clothing, and driving habits. Although you may vary some details, your habits allow you the freedom to structure your life with a minimum of attention to ordinary details. This gives you more time for planning new activities and making decisions.

Many personal habits are desirable and beneficial. Sometimes you may overlook giving a warm "thank you" for good things that your partner practices regularly, just because she or he loves and cares for you. Telling your partner what you enjoy gives more information than complaining about what you do not like. If you know what your partner likes, then you know what you can do that will bring pleasure. By contrast, if you know only what your partner does not like, then more searching is necessary to discover what she or he likes. Information from you is beneficial to your partner, just as you need your partner's feedback.

Habits Speak Loudly

What are your personal habits communicating to your spouse and to others? Often a person is not aware of how a specific pattern affects her or his partner in marriage. Taking time to examine your behavior routines is an important step toward greater understanding and love. Your mutual acceptance of each other can form the support for changing troublesome habits. You can enhance your relationship by talking about habits that you and your partner like.

Sometimes partners have different ways of doing things. It may be important to you that your partner accept certain habits, rather than asking you to give up what you feel is a part of your individuality. Your partner may feel the same way about some of your requests. One helpful approach is to clarify together the ways a habit or behavior causes a problem for the other partner. Then consider what you can do differently that will eliminate the problems and at the same time preserve your individualities.

Growing in Love Through Marriage

Christian marriage offers nurture and growth. The inner qualities of each person are expressed in the way that he or she treats others. Usually an individual's behavior at home extends outward into the community, as suggested by the proverb quoted at the beginning of this chapter.

Your adult development is not complete at the time of your wedding, nor even after ten or twenty years of marriage. Your marriage is a lifetime laboratory, or workshop, in which you can help each other continue to grow, guided by your best understandings of God's wishes.

Knowing that you really accept each other, your expression of grace, you can grow beyond any feelings of guilt that yours is not a perfect marriage. Christian marriage assumes that each partner accepts full responsibility for creating love and trust in every situation. Persons remain in relationships that are enjoyable, uplifting, and supportive, but withdraw and leave when relationships are unpleasant and negative.

As spouses, your intention to support and love each other "until death" refers not so much to a length of time as to an attitude toward the way you live with each other. One by-product of unconditional covenant love is the permanence of the partnership. This fidelity in marriage is a matter of being faithful to God and, on this basis, of responding to your spouse with love and concern. Your solemn promise to love each other, when expressed in daily interactions, is your best guarantee of avoiding divorce. It is saying to your partner and the world that nothing will keep you from loving and caring for your spouse, so you can learn to love each other more completely in every situation you encounter.

EXPLORE 1.3B: How I Feel About My Partner's Habits

Use this checklist to show how you feel about each other's habits. Answer separately. Then compare answers and discuss details of your responses.

	Very Bothered	Sometimes Bothered	Usually Neutral	Sometimes Pleased	Very Pleased
punctuality, being on time	_____	_____	_____	_____	_____
appearance, dress, grooming	_____	_____	_____	_____	_____
forgetfulness	_____	_____	_____	_____	_____
suggestions my partner gives	_____	_____	_____	_____	_____
attention my partner gives me	_____	_____	_____	_____	_____
use of tobacco, alcohol, drugs	_____	_____	_____	_____	_____
driving habits	_____	_____	_____	_____	_____
sense of humor	_____	_____	_____	_____	_____
expressions of affection	_____	_____	_____	_____	_____
housekeeping, neatness	_____	_____	_____	_____	_____
openness, flexibility	_____	_____	_____	_____	_____
honesty, truthfulness	_____	_____	_____	_____	_____
respect for others and me	_____	_____	_____	_____	_____
care of property	_____	_____	_____	_____	_____
care of personal belongings	_____	_____	_____	_____	_____
money habits	_____	_____	_____	_____	_____
encouraging me	_____	_____	_____	_____	_____
cooperation, consideration	_____	_____	_____	_____	_____
conversational speech skills	_____	_____	_____	_____	_____
swearing, slang, jargon	_____	_____	_____	_____	_____
sleep habits	_____	_____	_____	_____	_____
daily scheduling	_____	_____	_____	_____	_____
food and eating habits	_____	_____	_____	_____	_____
other: _____	_____	_____	_____	_____	_____

As you compare your responses, describe details of habits that you would like to modify. Some possibilities are:

• sleep habits, such as time to bed, time to rise, ability to go without sleep or naps, and sleep required
• speech habits, including talking too little, too much, too fast or slow
• eating habits, including food preferences, cooking styles, places to eat, table manners, and meal schedules

1.4

VALUES, CHOICES

Forgetting what lies behind and straining forward to what lies ahead, I press on toward the goal for the prize of the heavenly call of God in Christ Jesus.   *(Philippians 3:13-14, NRSV)*

You shape your marriage by the choices you make. Choices express your values. Recognizing these from the past enables you to commit to values that encourage growth for making your present and future.

Choosing Where You Want to Go

As partners, you make your relationship what it is. Together, you have the opportunity to shape your lives and to grow in directions that you intentionally choose. In this process you will find many opportunities to express your love as you deepen your understanding of yourselves and of others.

You and your partner are very important to each other, to your families and friends, to the church, to the community around you, and to God. You are unique, and your relationship is special and unique.

There is no one right way for you to create your marriage, yet there are basic communication processes that enable you to make your marriage succeed.

Together, you shape your relationship in your own ways. Through this growth you can share the fruits of God's Spirit: love, joy, peace, patience, kindness, generosity, faithfulness, gentleness, and self-control (Galatians 5:22-23, NRSV). Your marriage can be a means of grace and love, for yourselves and for others.

Spouses as Neighbors

Your partner in marriage is also your closest neighbor and friend. Although many others have important places in each of your lives, in marriage you vow to put each other first, before all other persons and things (Genesis 2:4). You continue to care about each other in happy and unhappy times. As you learn to care more about yourself, you are more able to love your partner.

These basic intentions are continually present in your lives—reaffirmed and modified daily by what you do and by how you treat each other. As you covenant together in marriage, each partner can say, "I expect to love and affirm you, and I anticipate that you will love and affirm me."

The Value of Loving

The results you want from your choices of goals, resources, and actions represent the expectations that you hold when things go right for you.

Love includes affection, warmth, care, concern, attention, and other pleasant events. The values aspect of expectations refers to the things that bring happiness, pleasure, and satisfaction to yourself and/or others.

Standards also appear in the events you would like to avoid because they are painful, disappointing, hurtful, or sad. You each decide whether a specific event is important or unimportant; whether it is pleasurable or painful; and whether you desire it or not.

A central affirmation of the wedding vows is that each spouse intends to be positively supporting to her or his partner under all circumstances and conditions. Each spouse promises to give unconditional love to the other—to care about the other, especially when it is difficult to do. Each partner also intends to accept the love, care, and support that his or her spouse offers. Although no couple fulfills this expectation perfectly, this covenant of mutual giving and receiving is a foundation of Christian marriage.

A basic guide for human relationships is the great commandment to "love the Lord your God . . . and . . . love your neighbor as yourself" (Mark 12:30-31; Matthew 22:37; Luke 10:25-28; based on Deuteronomy 6:4-5 and Leviticus 19:18). This loving affirmation is freeing and exciting, as well as perhaps overwhelming, mysterious, and difficult. Your covenant to value and love each other provides the foundation for accomplishing everything else in your relationship.

Based on the importance (or value) you assign to persons, events, and situations, you make choices that affect your future. In this way you choose your future. If your basic value is love and care for your partner and others, then you are choosing a future in which you give priority to the needs of others and yourself.

Value Loving as the Basis of Your Marriage

Your continued acceptance and basic affirmation of self and of each other underlies how you view everything that happens in your marriage. If you feel good about yourself, you are more likely to assume that things will work out well for you. You also are more likely to be independent and able to live happily on your own. As you join together in marriage, you can bring your strengths into a cooperative relationship that encourages more love.

Discounting Oneself

Many serious difficulties arise when a person discounts or devalues him or herself. When a person feels unloved, unwanted, rejected, or inadequate, he or she then may set up unrealistic hopes that the partner in marriage will provide most of what seems to be missing in life. The discounted person then expects the partner to give the love and meaning that the unloved person feels she or he has missed.

This is a heavy burden to place upon another person, even if that person is one's spouse. It sets the stage for disillusionment and disappointment, because no partner can always be giving in every situation. It is unhealthy to expect one spouse to be an all-loving parent, or a super servant who caters to the other's every need and wish. Obviously, if both partners come to marriage anticipating that the other will provide all the happiness, they are certain to find disappointment and emptiness.

You Are Loved!

Even when we discount ourselves, there is always hope. In every relationship, each partner has times when she or he wants to be cared for—to be valued by the other. These times need to be balanced with times when each partner gives love, warmth, and care. Your marriage offers you the opportunity to grow in love. You can begin to value yourself by accepting your partner's love for you and by thanking your partner for that love. This points to the power to act in loving ways as a second aspect of expectations.

To Tell All or Not?

As you share these topics together, there are two gifts that you can give to your partner. The first gift is respect for the other's privacy, which is the kindness of not prying out more than your partner is ready to share. The second gift is listening without judging, which expresses your love when you receive your

---

EXPLORE 1.4A: Affirm Each Other

Warm and sincere affirmation of each other is extremely important in your relationship. Take a few moments now to express your love to your partner using statements such as these:

Because I love you, I want to do what is best for you, for me, and for us.

I know you mean well for me when you _____.

I like the way you _____.

When you are close to me, I feel _____.

Because we care for each other, we can explore our expectations without fear.

partner's confidence as a shared gift—neither right nor wrong, but very real for both of you.

In this context, how much of your past should you tell your partner? Is it necessary for you to confess everything? Probably not, although this sometimes may be difficult to decide. Here are some guidelines.

If you wonder whether you should tell your partner something that is uncomfortable or embarrassing for you, consider whether the past event can in some way directly affect your partner or your relationship now. Is the event likely to become known to your partner anyway?

Is telling your partner a way of putting him or her down, or of making yourself feel less guilty?

If the event is not likely to affect your current relationship, it may be best to postpone telling about it. If you continue to be worried, discuss the situation with your mentor couple, minister, or a counselor in order to clarify what you want to tell and what you prefer to keep private.

Personal privacy is a right of each partner in marriage. As you gain confidence in each other's acceptance and love, you can comfortably share more of your past. However, part of our mystery as individuals is that we never can share everything about ourselves fully with another person—even with our spouse. God still loves you in your privacy and in your relationships.

With gifts that differ according to the grace given to us, let us use them . . . (Romans 12:9)

Please Do That Again . . . I Like It!

Expressing positive feelings toward your partner creates warmth and a common unity that strengthens your lives together. When you share positive feelings, you not only tell your partner how you feel about her or him, but you also are saying, "I like you and what you are doing . . . please do that again." These positive feelings include love, care, concern, happiness, pleasure, joy, and acceptance.

You can express positive feelings of care and affection in many ways by smiling, touching, and talking with your spouse. Being on time for appointments and planning time together show appreciation for each other. You show you care when you help your partner reach her or his goals. Sexual activities also are opportunities to share positive feelings, and humor and laughter express your joy and satisfaction.

You strengthen your common commitment as a couple by finding your healthy balance between past and current factors in your relationship. The dialogue in Explore 1.4C highlights the two extremes of past versus present. After reading it discuss your assumptions about how you will utilize past and present influences in your marriage.

EXPLORE 1.4B: Positive Feelings and Self-Esteem

Self-esteem is feeling good about oneself. Your sense of self-esteem (or self-worth) is closely related to the positive feelings that others express toward you.

Your experiences, both past and present, influence how you feel about yourself and your spouse. Talk about each of these sources and how you express positive feelings toward others.

How did family members express positive feelings toward each other? How did they react toward you? Describe some examples to your partner and compare the way each of your families communicated support, acceptance, love, and appreciation toward you.

Name some persons who have helped you build confidence in yourself, thus improving your sense of self-worth. Talk with your partner about some specific ways others have encouraged you. What common themes do you discover as you compare your experiences?

Describe to your partner some things she or he does that help you to feel good about yourself. Give some words and phrases that express positive feelings you would like to share with your partner.

At which times would you like your partner to express more care or support for you? As your partner asks for your affection and support, show or describe the positive feelings you have for him or her.

Talk about a recent time when you and your partner laughed heartily together.

EXPLORE 1.4C: Past Versus Present—Contrasting Views

The first part of a conversation between two spouses is given below. Partner A believes that background is more important than personality in influencing their marriage. Partner B thinks personality, habits, attitudes, and values are more influential for the couple's marital success.

Read the dialogue aloud together, with one partner reading the "A" statements and the other person reading the "B" statements. Try to reach a satisfying conclusion about the way your own backgrounds and personalities affect your relationship now.

A: If we can have a marriage just like my parents have, we really will be successful.

B: Their marriage is nice, but we are different from your parents and from my family. I think what we do with each other now is most important.

A: The way we treat each other now is mostly because of the way our families have treated us.

B: But my family wasn't always happy. My parents divorced when I was young. It's tough to be a single parent. I would hate to think that our marriage would be like that.

A: My parents have done so much for me. The way I can repay them is by being just like them. I guess I am what I have been.

B: I think my family would want me to improve on the way they did things. My attitudes are different from theirs. My kids shouldn't have to continue doing something just because I did it that way in the past.

A: Sure, but it's hard to change. When you suggest that I modify some of my habits, I think you don't understand how much my background influences me.

B: It seems that you value your family experiences and the friends you had while you were growing up. I'm glad you do. I just don't want to be stuck with the past and my mixed-up relatives. I have my own beliefs, and I want to do things our way, not the way someone else did.

A: Why change something, if it is good as it is? You sound as if you want to do everything differently. Do you want me to forget everything I have learned to value?

B: Of course not, but I do want us to grow and to be aware of what we do to and for each other now. It might help if we could talk about some specifics of our pasts and our personalities and the way they affect us now.

A: That's a good idea. In that way, we could decide which things we would like to keep and which we want to create for ourselves.

Continue your discussion together concerning other issues.

THEME TWO

HOPE AS VISION FOR YOUR JOURNEY

Visions of Hope

We always give thanks to God for all of you, constantly remembering before our God and Father your work of faith and labor of love and steadfastness of hope in our Lord Jesus Christ.

(1 Thessalonians 1:2-3, NRSV)

The marriage of Name *and* Name *unites their families and creates a new one. They ask for your blessing. Will all of you, by God's grace, do everything in your power to uphold and care for these two persons in their marriage? Eternal God . . . enable them to grow in love and peace with you and with one another all their days, that they may reach out in concern and service to the world, through Jesus Christ our Lord. Send therefore your blessing upon* Name *and* Name *that they may surely keep their marriage covenant, and so grow in love and godliness together that their home may be a haven of blessing and peace . . . Go to serve God and your neighbor in all that you do.*

—from the "Service of Christian Marriage," The United Methodist Hymnal, *pages 864-69*

Where do we grow from here? . . . Expectations are never quite the same as reality.

Please tell me you love me again. . . It's always so nice to hear.

EXPLORE 2: Some Definitions of Hope for Your Lifelong Journey

How do you define *hope*? How do you feel about your relationship? As you consider your faith commitment, communication power, resources, and love relationships, how do you feel about your marriage and your future? Your overall perspectives combine to form your hope for your future.

There are many ways to define hope in relation to your lifelong journey for you. In the following list, independently circle the words that best define hope. Then talk together regarding your choices. Add other phrases as needed.

happy	excited	positive	successful	uncertain
eager	anticipation	optimistic	puzzled	worried
fearful	sad	ecstatic	confident	secure
pessimistic	open	pleased	joy	vision

2.1

VISIONS, GOALS, TRANSITIONS

Marriage is a couple agreeing to conduct life in ways they both like . . .

Your wedding is for a day, yet your marriage is your lifelong journey together. Exchanging vows at your wedding ceremony is simple compared with the work and the joy of making your vows real in your daily lives together. Whether you are now anticipating your wedding or have already been married for months or years, this theme of hope invites you to take an overall, long-term perspective on your marriage. This includes the other three themes of faith, love, and power as you consider your future together.

One way of knowing your hope is in the big question: Overall, how happy, pleased, and satisfied are you with your marriage? When you are pleased with what you are experiencing, you have hope that it will continue at least as good as now, if not better. If you are unhappy with the present, you more likely will be fearful or worried about what you see as an unpleasant future.

Marriage continually brings many changes in your lives. Change, either planned or unplanned, creates stress. Stress gives you the opportunity to work toward mutually satisfactory solutions to any issues, whether new or old, that arise.

In your lifelong marital journey you apply your faith vision (commitment), power processes (competencies), and love relationships (care) across the stages of your marriage. To learn to love more completely, continually practice love with each other. As you build your home through your relationships, it becomes your home base, your soul's home, full of grace and peace, your haven for renewal.

Ups and Downs Are Normal

It is reassuring to remember that every successful couple has differences of opinions and occasional conflicts. Your sincere commitment to stay together and to work on troublesome issues is only the beginning chapter in your relationship. The joy of being together in warm and reassuring moments makes your efforts worthwhile. This combination of commitment and satisfaction probably is the difference between couples who succeed in marriage and those

---

EXPLORE 2.1A: Ups and Downs

Take some quiet time together to look at your total relationship since you met or during the past several months.

Half-way down on a sheet of paper, draw a horizontal line and mark it to indicate specific months or years. Above this line represents positive satisfying times (ups) and below this line are the negative unhappy times (downs). Then let each partner independently draw another line or make marks, as on a graph, to show the way you view your relationship during each time period.

When you have completed your lines, compare how you each see each time period. Note the down periods and the special up periods. Compare your perspectives and talk about factors that made each time down or up times.

---

who give up. Building on the positives in your marriage lays the foundation for facing the negatives honestly and with hope.

In a short-range view, a specific event may make your marriage appear to be going down. However, when you and your partner take a larger view, you may find that many good things are happening; and your overall perspective may be sometimes up, sometimes down, and sometimes steady.

As a married couple, you can give yourselves permission to disagree and to have your ups and downs. Each partner can also be open to accept the apology, forgiveness, and warmth of the other.

Marriage, in large measure, is a self-fulfilling prophecy, going in the direction that the two spouses take it. This means that in your marriage, you more or less produce what you expect to happen. Your resources, attitudes, and skills for communicating love and solving problems are essential tools you use to create the quality of marriage you would like. In many ways, you and your partner are really on your own. At times this may seem frightening, yet you can reach out to comfort and support each other as you develop. You may agree you will never go to sleep while you are angry. You may not solve the problem that night, but you can agree to talk about it later. You can give praise and thanks for everything that strengthens you in your marriage, and you can pray for insight and wisdom concerning areas where you still need to grow.

Goals are your standard for evaluating your satisfaction, happiness, and success in your marriage journey. You use feedback from your journey to recommit to your marriage and make course corrections. Deciding whether your marriage is happy or satisfying involves matching what is happening (reality) to your expectations/wants/ dreams (goals). To increase your happiness, you modify your actions or your goals, or usually some of both.

A Long-Range View

There are many issues that newly married couples face in the first few months. It is helpful to take a long-range view of your years ahead in order to put daily events into a better perspective.

During your married life, you and your partner will experience several definite periods. After many years, it may even seem you have had three or four marriages to each other because you both are changing and growing in love.

Sometimes you may wish your spouse were like she or he used to be. Of course, this is not possible because of the growth within yourselves and the changes in others, your career, work, and in the world around you.

Expect changes in the way you each view your marriage. Together you can take control of the ways you cope with these and continue to make your marriage healthy and enjoyable. You will know you are growing in love when you improve the quality of your relationships with your spouse, your family, and others around you. Even though we are not perfect, we can be more familiar and comfortable with each other the longer we are together. What are you doing to build friendship with your spouse, stretch your boundaries, and prevent boredom? Long-term success in your marriage means you intend to make your marriage work.

Crises: Expecting the Unexpected

Together, the days you shape add up to the years of marriage you will share. Across those years, you can expect some changes to produce unexpected crises. A crisis is not the event itself, but your interpretation of the event.

A crisis may be the loss of a job, death of a loved one, divorce, moving, or other changes. Usually when a crisis occurs, you have reached a point where you cannot cope well with this one additional situation. What happens is important, but your reactions to the happening are even more critical in relation to the outcome.

In most of life's events, partners have a sense of being in control. In a crisis, when it seems as if you have lost control of your life and your marriage, you still have the power to turn a crisis into a time for growth. This is done by using your skills and working with your partner and others who can help you. Sometimes you may need to pull back from events for a while so you can regroup your resources and cope more effectively with life.

Having a Dual-Control Marriage

A dual-control marriage suggests two key factors in your marriage: joint warmth, affection, and love; and individual control, power, skills, and abilities. A dual-control marriage, like a dual-control electric blanket, provides the desired warmth for each partner, yet each partner is able to adjust the settings for maximum comfort as she or he perceives it. You each express affection and control in every encounter, conversation, and event of your marriage. You and your partner can be in control of your future together. By identifying what you consider to be good and desirable, you then can decide how you will reach those desired goals. This is tremendously freeing and exciting because it means you can choose to stay together, just as you might choose to separate. Together, in your dual-control marriage, you can blend your lives as you please.

Wife and Husband as Coequal Leaders of the Household

Our deeper understanding of the equality of men and women today emphasizes wife and husband as equal partners who give unqualified love to each other. Together you choose models for your marriage that will allow you to express covenant love most fully. Your model may differ from others, but when unconditional love is present, nearly any model can be a genuine expression of Christian marriage.

Marriage may be described as the joining of two persons into "one flesh." In one Creation story this statement appears: "Therefore a man leaves his father and his mother and cleaves to his wife, and they become one flesh. And the man and his wife were both naked, and were not ashamed" (Genesis 2:24-25, RSV).

Today we may infer that a parallel also applies—namely, that a woman also leaves her parents and cleaves to her husband. The intent, however, is clear. When a woman and a man covenant in marriage, their first loyalty is to each other, and all other loyalties follow afterward. "Two becoming one flesh, unit, or corporate body, yet two persons" in marriage illustrates the richness of God's offering to us.

"One flesh" implies much more than sexual inter-course, although those expressions of love are included in the expression. Important as sex is, it takes more than sexual interest to maintain a marriage. Common goals, the same residence, affection and personal needs, and relations with relatives and friends all are involved in the covenant of marriage.

Perhaps the term *body* may better express today this broader meaning of one flesh, in that marriage resembles a legal corporate body that functions as one unit, yet has two individual members.

Some use "one flesh" to suggest that spouses are to think alike, act alike, always agree, do everything together, and become carbon copies of each other. On the contrary, into the one corporate body of marriage, wife and husband bring a uniqueness that enriches both. Christian marriage assumes that both have equal rights and responsibilities.

Marriage is the unique way in which man and woman encounter each other and discover the fullness of the mystery of being feminine and masculine. The husband represents all men, and the wife represents all women. Thus a valid marriage is to have one woman and one man so that both genders are uniquely present to each other in each marriage. Any other household arrangement is not a marriage, although such arrangements may enable a household to operate as a domestic unit in society.

Faith, Hope, Home

Your faith commitments define your marriage, which in turn shapes your home, your household system, and your daily patterns. Marriage is the key relationship in the family because the husband and wife shape the structure, priorities, and atmosphere of others in their household system. Your home is like a domestic church, or "microchurch," that operates twenty-four hours each day, seven days every week. The ways you live constantly express your faith and influences your faith and future. Faith, church, and home are interlaced daily in mutual support.

At minimum, every home should be safe, free from physical and verbal violence, and cause no harm to

---

EXPLORE 2.1B: Your Household

Talk together about your current household and the persons who live there. If you are not yet married, how will you change your home base after your wedding? If you are now married, how have you changed your home since your wedding? If you have been living together before your wedding, how will your home change? How do you want your household to be similar and/or different from your childhood home(s)?

anyone in it. Every home should respect all persons involved, affirm truth and honesty, and encourage caring, sharing, and equal rights and responsibilities. Every home needs to have clearly defined structures, boundaries, and guidelines, yet be flexible, forgiving, and open to feedback from all involved. In these ways spouses share their faith, love, hope, and power.

Your covenant faith as spouses defines your home. It also enables you as parents to give your children security and flexibility as you launch them from childhood into life as adults. No matter who is living in your household, your marriage is the foundation for structuring your home relationships.

Values and Goals

A value is the worth and importance that you assign to a certain belief, activity, or event. Positive values are the virtues you support and live. A goal is an objective you set for yourself based on what you judge as most important. You then choose actions that will enable you to reach your goal.

When you say that you are happy or satisfied or successful, you probably mean that you are reaching your goals. Some goals may be short range while others may extend much farther into the future, such as creating a successful marriage or succeeding in work.

You each bring your personal standards and goals to your relationship. You may also bring some values and goals of persons you admire. Your beliefs and goals fit together when they are similar. If you hold different standards, you may achieve personal goals without infringing on each other's objectives. Goal conflicts challenge you and your partner to find a mutually satisfactory compromise or cooperative solution.

Your actions express your priorities and goals. The way you spend your time and money indicates the things you really value.

EXPLORE 2.1C: Clarifying Your Goals

First, answer these questions about your values and goals. Answer independently. Use this code to show how important each goal or value is for you:

4 = essential for me
3 = very important for me

2 = somewhat important for me
1 = not important for me

Woman   Man

1. Help to eliminate racial, sex, or other prejudices
2. Please my parents, friends, or others
3. Get more education
4. Help others who are having difficulties
5. Be successful in my career
6. Learn another language or other communication skill
7. Have children of our own or adopt children
8. Be active in volunteer community work or service clubs
9. Participate in church activities
10. Have leisure time for hobbies, arts, sports, vacations

After you have answered, transfer your answers to the same sheet so you can compare and discuss your answers. Which of these goals is most important to you? Which are least important? How similar are your values and goals? On which goals do you disagree? What are your essential agreements for you to have a good marriage?

Give some examples of what you meant in making your choices.

Finding the Real You

At each stage in your marriage in every communication and event, there is always one more layer of meaning and intention underneath the layer you express. As you reach through these layers you learn more about yourself and your spouse. Your covenant commitment is essential to provide the security, safety, acceptance, and freedom to search the depths of your beings and grow in love. This is a major reason for our emphasis upon your covenant in marriage.

EXPLORE 2.1D Affirmations

Read the following statement aloud to each other to show how you each affirm your spouse.

I want the best for you, for me, and for us. If it does not seem that way in this event, then I'll try again. Down deep, I really do love and care for you, for me, for us, and for others. I accept you as you really are now. This is what I mean when I say that "I love you."

Family Stages

For couples who have children, family stages relate to the ages of the children—especially the oldest and the youngest child. Couples who are experiencing pregnancy or the excitement of preschool children will enjoy associating with others who are in the same general stage. They can swap stories, share child care, and exchange toys and clothes. In this way they provide mutual support in learning about and coping with parenting.

Marriage transitions often occur when the first child enters elementary school, when children reach adolescence, when the last child enters school, and when the last child graduates. Many details of these stages are available in the reference listing in this guidebook.

Stages in your marriage may also be marked by major job and career changes, a move from one community to another, the death of a close relative or special friend, or by significant changes in your health. Your career-stage cycles interact with your marriage stages, but none of these is a final determination of your happiness. You and your partner can use these challenges to strengthen your relationship.

Planning Ahead

A stage consists of many events during that period in your lives. Your expectations and goals guide you toward some events and away from others according to your values and needs.

Be clear about the events and expectations each of you considers to be most significant because you probably will act on them. How you picture your future shapes your marriage today.

Stages and Changes to Anticipate

Crises and changes become less threatening when you take a long-range view of your marriage. Many family and adult development specialists describe our adult years as a series of stages with special experiences that tend to take place at each stage.

Stages in marriage typically are related to the personal experiences of each partner, the partners' stage of career development, and the ages of their children, if any. Your calendar age is less important than the types of events occurring in your lives. There is nothing magic about age thirty or age forty. However, if you believe that life is over for you when you leave age twenty-nine, or age thirty-nine, then you may perceive that birthday as a crisis.

The more important issue is whether you are where you want to be and who you want to be, at each stage of your life and of your marriage. Again, your judgment of your success depends upon whether your real life experiences match your expectations. Your marriage relationship is always independent of other life events, yet may be affected by them.

EXPLORE 2.1E: Your Timelines

Together, draw a very long line to represent the time from now until your retirement, or beyond—the rest of your life. Along your line, mark some important events that each of you hopes will have happened by the time you reach a certain age. Some of these may be joint events and others may affect only one partner.

Then add other probable events that may influence your marriage. Some of these might be the things your parents or other relatives may be doing by the time you reach a particular age. Some markers may be alternative, or second-choice, goals. Your timeline might look something like this one.

Ages:	20s	30s	40s	50s	60s & beyond

- Complete educations
- Big trip before children come
- Coming of children
- Move to "permanent" residence
- All the children are now in school
- Becoming more active in community affairs
- Career advancements
- Another move to improve career status
- Wondering whether it is all worth it
- Possible changes in career/work
- Doing more things as a couple
- Last child graduates from school
- Period of maximum income
- Becoming grandparents/grandpeople
- It really is worth the effort!
- Retirement/Reengagement

These examples of phrases to identify periods in your lives are more general than yours will be. As you talk about your future, try to be specific about what you want or do not want to happen at each age.

Discuss your feelings about looking at your whole lives together. Share dreams, hopes, and desires. At times, hug and touch each other as you talk.

2.2

MARRIAGE, CHURCH, WORLD

If there is righteousness in the heart,
there will be beauty in the character.
If there is beauty in the character,
there will be harmony in the home.
If there is harmony in the home,
there will be order in the nation.
When there is order in each nation,
there will be peace in the world.
We believe the source of it all is God.
(Based on an old Chinese proverb)

The whole world is at your door. What will you do? Like ripples in a pond of water, others affect you in many ways just as your marriage reaches out to influence the lives of many others. With all its privacy and intimacy, marriage is also a social affair because it is part of the larger social systems in the world around you. You are part of your neighborhood, your community, city, state, and nation. Increasingly events anywhere in the world directly impact you through mass media, internet, travel, and business.

Some of these involvements with others, such as paying taxes and conforming to acceptable behaviors, are required. Some are necessities, such as traveling on public streets. Some are privileges, such as voting or driving a vehicle. You choose whether to be a part of many other activities in your community and in the world. Among these are your community and recreational interests, celebrations, church life, and faith expressions.

Everyone Is Everywhere!

The rhythms and polarities of marriage transport you and your partner from intimate sexual and personal intercourse to social intercourse with the whole world. Living happily ever after cannot be done in isolation from others. Your marriage expresses your personalities. Through the lens of your marriage, you can see other persons with new

vision, and choose the ways you will relate to them. In marriage, partners can be everything to each other only for brief periods. You need others, and they need you.

Community, Leisure, and Recreation

You may choose to use your free time in community, recreational, and other leisure activities. You may use it to relax, to help others, and as an opportunity for personal growth and education.

Become involved in activities that make your community a better place to live. Some may be causes that are important to you, such as environmental concerns, alternate energy sources, or health improvement. You may help your community by leading an organized group of children or youth or as part of a church or community agency. You may take part in political, labor, management, or civic committees. Through volunteering as individuals or as a couple, you join with others to make your community a better place in which to live and meet new friends with similar interests and values.

Recreation includes individual and group sports, hobbies, crafts, and other interests that offer enjoyable new experiences. These are ways you re-create yourself. Some, such as tennis, require two people, while others, such as fishing or bicycle riding, can be done alone. Some types of recreation require travel and may be expensive, while others can be done at home or may cost nothing.

Leisure refers to all your free time—the time when you are not working at your job. In addition to the time you invest in your community and in recreation, each partner needs some personal time. Take time to relax, rest, or do nothing. It can be used for couple, family, and friendship activities. Leisure can be an opportunity for meditation and self-renewal.

Through your church you participate in a community of Christians who are committed to God in Christ and who share interests concerning worship, education, social action, and family values. Your church offers you a special window to the world so you can know the world in ways that are alternate to the secular media views. By participating as a couple in fellowship classes, groups, and committees you receive support as you minister to others and serve the world's needs.

EXPLORE 2.2A: Leisure Activities

Allow time to discuss the way you each use your leisure time. Here are some possible areas to consider:

1. In which community service activities do you participate? What would you like to do for your community?

2. How much money do you spend on recreation, sports, and hobbies compared to giving to charitable, service, and community causes? Do you agree on these expenses?

3. Which of your recreational activities help to maintain or improve your health? In what ways? Does your health or physical condition limit your recreational activities? How have you adjusted to these limitations?

4. What do you enjoy for hobbies, crafts, arts, or recreation? First, let one partner describe the activities you think the other enjoys; then let the other partner comment on the description.

5. When do you enjoy being alone? How much time should be personal time for each of you to do things separately? What are your arrangements for personal time? When do you enjoy being with others?

6. Describe the way you would like to change your use of leisure time. How do you cope with job and career obligations that would reduce your time for leisure?

7. What will be your legacy as a couple? How can God use your unique gifts as a couple to further God's kingdom?

Family Religion

Prayers, devotionals, Bible readings, and hymns are important as part of Christian nurture in your home. Even more essential are your regular and consistent expressions of love, kindness, consideration, and other "fruits of God's Spirit" since your behaviors demonstrate your faith in action. You live your faith in God through your intimate daily contacts. This is active religion.

There are many forces that pull spouses and family members in different directions, but commitment to common values, virtues, and religious faith helps to unite the family in worship and lifestyle patterns. We encourage you both to agree to participate in the same religious tradition and to be active in the same congregation.

Different Faith Traditions

If you each hold to a different religious denomination or faith, such as Methodist-Baptist, Protestant-Catholic, Christian-Jew, Christian-Muslim, or other combination, then it is vital for you to find as much agreement as possible concerning prayers, worship, and lifestyle in your home. If one partner wants certain faith expressions and the other does not care or is opposed, then how will (or do) each of you feel about your partner's faith perspectives? Find agreements that respect both spouses and implement them in your family lifestyle.

You may both consider yourselves "not religious" or opposed to faith expressions, yet the ways you act do express your values, whether helpful or harmful. At least seek to identify the values and priorities you hold in common and mutually support each other in living these in your home.

Teach your children the best you know about life and how to live it. This is your real faith. As your children see you regularly caring for others, being considerate, truthful, and honest, they come to value what you encourage and consistently repeat it. As they see you praying and leading worship in your home, they realize its importance and want to take turns with you. Your children will copy whatever you do. From childhood through adolescence they gradually assume more responsibility for their own faith commitments and actions. They take your actions as their model for their ways to grow and live.

Expressing Your Social Faith: Church Possibilities

The church is God's witness in today's world, supporting the best in life and calling attention to the needs of persons and groups. In this age of technology, leisure, professionalism, and self-interest, God continues to call the church to its servant existence. As individuals, as couples, and as families, you continually are called to be a part of God's exciting work today; you are invited to invest your lives.

Jesus pointed to the excitement and joy of a wedding to describe the importance of continuing our relationship with God and with one another in the Christian community of faith. For example, "The kingdom of God may be compared to a king who gave a wedding banquet for his son" (Matthew 22:2, NRSV). When we participate in Christian fellowship, we are joining with God in celebrating life and growing in love so the Christian community becomes the body of Christ in service to the world.

Religion and church involvement have unique meanings for each of you. Since a local church is both a religious and a social organization, it provides important ways for you to develop friendships, become involved in your community, and worship God.

Your religious background and church activity probably fit into one of these categories: partners from different Protestant denominations; one partner Protestant, the other Roman Catholic, Jewish, or other religious tradition; one partner from

---

EXPLORE 2.2B: World Concerns

In the process of looking at important personal, couple, and family issues, it is easy to overlook some of the major concerns that face us all as part of the world community. Take time to talk about these and similar questions:

1. What proportion of the world's resources are rightfully yours as a couple, if you are concerned about couples and families everywhere?

2. Have you considered how much of the world's energy you use? How much of it is from nonrenewable sources, such as petroleum? How much of your residence and transportation energy comes from renewable sources, such as water or solar power?

3. How do you feel about the overpopulation and intense hunger of people in many areas of the world? What are you doing about these or other needs of other families?

4. What are your community, national, or world concerns, as you and your partner consider your jobs, money, and possessions? In your responses to these concerns, how does your view on Christian stewardship make a difference?

a church tradition, the other not involved in any religious group; and neither partner involved in any religious group. Consider the ways your previous religious experiences affect your decisions about your church involvement as a couple. Examine how your present church activity (or lack of it) may be in reaction to hurtful experiences in your childhood.

It is important that you both be involved in a local church in your community. Your involvement with others in a parish will call you out of selfish isolation. Your genuine love as a couple will lead you to share your lives with others. As a by-product, participation in the church can enrich your own relationship as well.

EXPLORE 2.2C: Ways You Express Faith

Allow time when you can talk together about your personal faith. Some of these questions may help you to share these areas with each other:

In what ways do you participate in the Christian community now? As a couple, what kind of church involvement do you have and/or would you like?

Will (or do) you participate in the same local church? When both partners are not active in the same church, they miss opportunities to be together and to develop friendships with other couples who share similar beliefs and standards.

Here are some types of group involvement that could be expressions of your personal faith. Describe how you would like to be involved in some of these.

1. Sunday worship and church school classes or groups
2. study and fellowship groups in church
3. church committees and work groups
4. health, welfare, and civic improvement groups
5. political parties and political action groups
6. the arts, charitable, scientific, and environmental causes
7. social clubs, fraternal orders, service clubs, secret orders
8. groups to help children, youth, seniors, disabled, disadvantaged

Talk about which of these you would like to take part in as a couple and which each partner would like to do individually. In what ways do these involvements express your personal faiths?

2.3

NEGATIVES: DISSATISFACTION, DIVORCE

A marriage doesn't just fall apart. . . . It takes a lot of little things to wear it down.

Every couple encounters dry times and periods of lack of romance in their marriage. Each day of your marriage you either move closer to your spouse and renew your romance or you move farther apart toward divorce. To stay happily married requires you to eliminate major negatives, such as violence, extramarital affairs, financial mismanagement, and addiction to drugs, alcohol, or gambling. Constant criticism, contempt, disrespect, emotional withdrawal, and refusing to acknowledge these negatives also move you toward divorce.

Couples may slip into routines that become boring, leaving them feeling empty and unappreciated. These patterns involve cycles and interactions that have several sources. Cycles and patterns are part of your marriage and home system. As you look at your lifestyle, find ways you can change your system and increase your satisfaction.

Cycles, patterns, and systems are givens in your marriage. Whether they produce negative or positive outcomes is up to you and your spouse. Recognize your cycles so you can plan ways to support positives.

Work and Home Interactions

Your work requirements produce cycles of being at work versus being at home and the stress and fatigue from work. Work patterns are a major factor in whether you are together or apart. Whether your work schedules for you and your spouse are the same each week, seasonal, or subject to change, try to recognize how these demands interact with your physiological cycles and scheduling time together. If your work requires long periods of time apart from each other, be alert to possible subtle shifts in the amount of power and control you each have in your marriage. The spouse who is home more may take control, feel lonely, or otherwise develop patterns that unintentionally shut out the other partner. Love notes and calls can keep you in tune with each other.

From Negatives to Positives

Who should take the first step when things are not going well in your marriage? Answer: both spouses.

EXPLORE 2.3A: How Are You Changing Your Patterns?

For each type of work-home cycle, describe a pattern you see and how you feel about it. How is each pattern related to your physiological, emotional, work, and other cycles?

What changes would you like to make? Which patterns do you enjoy and want to continue?

Consider the ways you transition from work when you return home, such as greeting each other and your children (if any), changing clothes, and preparing a meal. Which specific changes do you want to make? What responses (if any) do you dread as you come home? What do you welcome?

When you want your spouse to improve, it is up to you to make the first move. Your spouse's negative patterns developed in relation to your attitudes and behaviors. When you modify your own attitudes and behaviors, it is easier for your spouse to respond differently. Each day is a new day. As you are free to act in more caring ways, so is your partner. The person who wants things different begins with a new pattern. Even saying the same words with a warmer, more considerate tone of voice can be an effective way to start afresh.

Differences and disappointments are a normal part of every marriage. To cope with these, consider each difference and assign it to one of these categories:

- *differences that are not worth mentioning*, so you show your love to your partner by overlooking these minor habits or behaviors;
- *differences you cannot solve at the moment* because of circumstances or risk, so you hope to talk about them at some future time, possibly with a pastor or counselor;
- *differences you and your partner can discuss* comfortably and resolve immediately; and differences you anticipate, but may never be able to resolve.

This covenant approach signifies that you choose to stay together. You decide to love each other as you are, rather than requiring either partner change in order to have the other's love. This is the grace and unconditional acceptance you give to your partner that makes it safe for your partner to grow. Likewise, when your spouse accepts you unconditionally then you can drop your defenses and grow in love. From this perspective, disappointments can become opportunities for growth.

To resolve differences, you may revise your expectations, your behaviors, or both. Disagreements are a step toward establishing your personal and couple limits. Respect for genuine personal differences is an important factor in your lives together. Diverse perspectives keep partners alive, awake, and sensitive to each other, and dealing with them offers each of you the opportunity to affirm, forgive, and broaden your love. This deepening love can hold you together through rough, as well as in happy times. When you live this covenant, you are saying to your partner, "I care deeply about you, and I will continue to be here for you and with you."

Dreams and Hopes

Temptations to leave your marriage, whether real or imagined, challenge you to recommit yourself to your spouse. One benefit of your wedding and public registration of your marriage is to support you together when you face dry times of your journey and are tempted to quit. These external constraints keep you together in those times when you really do not feel like it. No couple can expect to stay on an emotional high all the time. To agree on a no-divorce attitude closes off any potential exits so you can learn how to grow in love and increase your intrinsic personal dedication reasons for commitment.

Some behaviors or habits of your mate may surprise, annoy, or disappoint you. By contrast, you may believe that none of your habits has a negative effect on your partner! Sometimes the unrealistic hope that marriage will solve all personal problems leads to criticism or dissatisfaction. It is important to keep your dreams up to date and talk with your partner about your feelings.

Building on the positive elements in your relationship helps to keep your marriage fresh and alive. You need leisurely times together when you can dream aloud about your future and share your hopes and wishes. An exciting mystery of marriage is the

---

EXPLORE 2.3B: Threats to Your Marriage

1. What types of persons or events might threaten your marriage or lead you to divorce?

2. When you feel you would like to leave your marriage, what do you do about it? In what way can you talk about this with your partner or with others?

3. Describe the greatest fear, worry, or concern you have about your marriage. Share how you feel about each other and try to eliminate the source of your fear.

4. Describe two or three hopes and dreams you have for your marriage. Talk about ways you can accomplish these in the next months or years.

continual awakening in each partner of the potential for love, growth, and new accomplishments. Sharing your hopes and dreams can bring you closer together and encourage greater teamwork in your marriage.

Coping With Feelings About Negatives

Negatives include personal feelings that separate us from others or that reduce our sense of self-worth. Negative feelings are not "bad" in the sense that you should ignore, suppress, or cover them up. They make us aware of dangers. These feelings are your way of saying to yourself and to others, "Something is wrong. I interpret this situation as threatening me in some way. When this happens, I feel angry, insecure, afraid, or sad."

Negative feelings also can be a way to say, "I care about you, and I don't want anything to come between us." Some of your negative feelings are temporary and will fade away as you and your partner go on to enjoy pleasant times together. You probably have other feelings that are more persistent. If these feelings continue in your relationship, you will need to find ways to express them and to cope constructively with their causes.

Negatives About Negatives

Negative feelings with which you respond to a specific situation or person are called primary feelings. You also have emotional responses to the feelings themselves. You may feel guilty about being angry, or you may feel sad about feeling alone.

To move beyond your secondary feelings, another person, such as your partner, needs to reach out to you and accept you and your primary feelings just as you are. The grace of your relationship is that both of you want to be fully aware of each other without repressing or covering up parts of yourself.

Negative feelings can be useful because they alert you to threats and strains that need to be modified in order to preserve yourself and your relationships with others. The communication skills you use to express positive feelings can be adapted to enable you to become aware of and to express negative feelings.

When negatives seem beyond your control, they will take over and destroy your marriage. Among these are violence, extramarital sexual involvements, and addictions to alcohol, drugs, gambling, sex, and other compulsive behaviors. Facing these serious unpleasant possibilities in marriage may be difficult

---

EXPLORE 2.3C: Negative Feelings

Arrange a relaxed time together to talk about the way you each handle your negative feelings. These questions may guide you:

1. How often do you each use flight, fight, and reorientation (summarized on page 45) to cope with threats and negative feelings? Describe to your partner a recent incident when you used one of these methods. If you could relive the situation, in what ways would you act differently?

2. With your partner, identify your negative feelings about a situation and attempt to trace them to possible underlying fears that you will be rejected, unloved, or devalued by the persons involved. Discuss together what you find. At what points did (do) you forgive your partner? When do you need to ask for your partner's forgiveness?

Tell your partner about a recent time when you realized that she or he really accepted you and your feelings and interpretations and allowed you to really be yourself.

3. Which are more difficult for you to express: negative feelings or positive feelings? What are some of your secondary feelings about other primary feelings—for example, feeling guilty about being happy?

4. Describe the way your family members express negative feelings. How did they express feelings when you were growing up?
• To what extent do (did) they strike things or persons, gripe, fuss, curse, nag, or complain?
• When were they passively aggressive by being cold, aloof, silent, or uncooperative?
• When did they calmly describe a situation and their negative feelings about it?
• Which of these do you now use with your partner?

It is easier for some couples to be more explicit when they write their answers to these questions.

and often requires the aid of capable professional help. Covenant love means you want to address these openly rather than assume they will never affect you.

Your covenant vow of marriage means neither spouse will let anything else stand in the way of growing in love for each other. Any behavior pattern that hurts either spouse in any way will eventually destroy your marriage if you do not effectively eliminate it.

Abuse and Violence

Every home is called to be a haven of blessing and place of peace. Positive peace includes having an absolute, unconditional no-violence agreement. No matter how much you disagree, or are angry, or feel cornered, you must agree that neither spouse will ever intentionally hurt the other. This eliminates physical, mental, and sexual abuse of any kind. It means that neither spouse will ever hit, slap, push, or otherwise hurt the other spouse or anyone else in the home.

Much is known today about the cycle of domestic violence. This cycle begins with increasing stress, culminates in physical hurts, followed by a time of making up, often including promises that it will never happen again (although it often does). The cycle

repeats as stresses increase, producing another time of violence.

Couples with many skills for positive problem solving may avoid violence by agreeing neither will ever hurt the other so both feel safe. Spouses whose family background include violence may also need professional assistance to replace violence, the weapon of last resort, with positive caring ways to cope with threats, stress, and disappointments.

Addictions: Alcohol, Drugs, Food, Gambling

Addiction to alcohol or other drugs means the addicted person places the drug as more important than the spouse. In many cases the spouse, perhaps unknowingly, may be a codependent or enabler.

Food addictions include avoidance of food, extreme overeating, and other types of eating disorders. Gambling, whether legal or not, is an attempt to get something for nothing.

Regardless of which spouse displays an addictive pattern, out of love both spouses cooperate to understand the sources of the problem and to find solutions that replace the negatives with constructive positive patterns.

EXPLORE 2.3D: Elephants in Your Home

Denying any addiction is like having an elephant living in your home but pretending not to notice it. Living in denial will eventually destroy your marriage.

Here are some major negatives that could destroy your marriage. Select one of these and randomly decide which spouse will roleplay having that negative and the other spouse roleplay responses to it. Then talk about how you each would cope with that problem to support your positive growth in your marriage. Consider these negatives:

Violence: physical, sexual, emotional
Addiction to alcohol, drugs, medications, food
Extramarital sexual involvement
Gambling, money mismanagement
Other addictions _____
Other negatives _____

If you currently face any of these negatives, or if your discussion should trigger feelings that are beyond your abilities to resolve, take steps to get professional help now.

Positives crowd out negatives. Describe positive behaviors and qualities that fill your home with joy and health and, as a by-product, prevent negatives from intruding and taking over your marriage. Talk about what you are now doing that crowds out each of these negatives.

What's Happening Now?

It is great to be alive, and being alive means change. Change is inevitable, but growth is intentional. Old habits, like old clothes, no longer fit as they did. In your growth as partners, the resources of support couples, your church, current friends, and others can help you as you continue in your life journey together. Because of your covenant as partners, you can look at problems and crises as challenges for growth.

In a conflict, partners often think that one must win and the other must lose. In most conflicts, however, it is possible for both to win by changing schedules, compromise, sharing goals, and planning.

Your goals and preferences will not always coincide with those of your partner. Agree to have room for differences and disagreements. Together you usually can resolve conflicts about specific issues when you both have a basic attitude toward yourselves and toward each other that is positive, caring, affirmative, and supportive and communication and problem-solving skills.

Every Street Has Some Bumps

Your road to marital happiness has several bumps and a few sharp curves. Some days may be stormy, icy, or frozen. Floods may wash out a bridge, or you may find unexpected detours that force you to vary your route. As one person said, "I took my partner for better or worse, but I didn't know it could be so much worse."

We believe that there are no problems big enough to destroy your relationship, unless in some way you decide to use a problem as a reason to separate.

This attitude of Christian love was expressed many times by the apostle Paul, for instance, in this statement "Let love be genuine . . . hold fast to what is good . . . rejoice in your hope, be patient in suffering, persevere in prayer" (Romans 12:9-12, RSV).

You and your partner can develop this attitude of forgiveness and love. Some issues may have roots in events that happened before you knew each other, and those problems may be severe enough to require professional help. Even a very healthy and stable person sometimes can be overwhelmed by difficulties.

As you grow through a crisis, you will discover your own strengths as individuals and as a couple. There are many resources in your church and community to assist you and your partner in resolving problems and dealing with crises.

EXPLORE 2.3E: Setting Limits

Take time now to explore the effects that some of the following difficulties might have on your relationship. Talk with your partner about these and other issues. Share your attitudes and feelings.

Keep asking yourselves, "Is there any conflict or problem that is so big, so unforgivable, so terrible, that you would leave your partner, whom you now love and enjoy?" Here are some issues to discuss:

- losing a job
- spending too much money
- loneliness or frustration
- spending too much time with your work
- adultery
- physical abuse
- unwillingness to talk about problems

Coping Strategies

There are three basic ways to cope with persons or situations to which you attach negative feelings:

Flight

Moving away from a threatening situation puts more distance between you. Physical distance is a protection against the threat, but sometimes emotional distance can provide a similar defense by changing your relation to the threat. Some examples of flight are turning your back, walking away, pouting, emotional withdrawal, coldness, depression, extramarital affairs, and staying away from home when it is not required. Fleeing from a threat restores your sense of safety by putting you farther away so the danger cannot reach you. However, it does not deal with the problem because flight reduces the contact you have with the other person(s) or thing(s) involved.

Fight

When you fight the threat, you move against the person or situation in an attempt to defend yourself and reduce its ability to hurt you. Hostile, aggressive behavior is your attempt to reduce the threatening power of the person or thing and to control it, to become safe and secure.

You may fight physically, verbally, or in more subtle ways. Fighting may be physical aggression, name calling, noncooperation, taking revenge, shouting, swearing, destroying property, and hurting oneself.

Reorientation

Some threats, along with your fear and anger toward them, will dissolve or disappear when you look at them from a different point of view. For example, the fear that you are lost disappears when you locate familiar markers. The fear of being alone can turn into joy when you realize that your partner really does care about you.

Sometimes you can remove threats by changing your expectations or your goals. Reorienting yourself to the situation is a constructive way for partners to deal with negative feelings. This enables you to continue in contact with each other and to develop the strength and skill to cope with threats to yourselves and your relationship. Negotiating positive agreements and problem solving are examples of reorientation.

EXPLORE 2.3F:
Check Your Strategies

For each of these basic coping styles describe a situation when it happened, what you did, and its impact on your partner. Then describe how you both want to work together to improve your coping styles.

Flight
  Situation
  What each did
  Improve by

Fight
  Situation
  What each did
  Improve by

Reorientation
  Situation
  What each did
  Improve by

Roleplay each improvement now and affirm each other for growing.

"Get My Way" Behaviors

Sometimes in conflict situations, partners respond in "get my way" behaviors. Some of these behaviors may be thought of as habits or typical emotional reactions. However, a closer look suggests they are used by individuals to manipulate their partners. The partner who uses "get my way" behaviors is seeking to control the other in some way. Often both partners may be playing these types of games at the same time. Some hurtful behaviors are pouting, crying, blaming someone else, and pretending to be helpless or shy. Some shout or swear in efforts to control their partners. In the extreme, one partner may strike or cause physical pain to the other.

Getting Professional Help

If you and your partner fail to find a satisfactory solution to a problem after you honestly have attempted to follow the problem-solving steps in Section 4.3, you still have some alternatives. You may consult your mentor couple or pastor, seek professional counseling, marriage therapy, financial consultation, or legal assistance. One good indication of your potential for growth is that you can agree to find help you need.

Go together as a couple, but if one is willing to seek help, it is still helpful for the other spouse to go. Often getting help to make changes in your own attitudes and behaviors will affect how the other person responds to you. If either or both of you do not want to seek help, this may be a sign that the future of your relationship is in serious trouble. If you are not sure how to ask for help, talk with your pastor, counselor, or a couple you trust to help clarify your concerns and find help to cope with challenges.

Marriage Counseling and Therapy

Seeking personal or marital counseling actually involves the first six steps of the problem-solving procedure described in Section 4.3.

Step 1: You and your partner agree on a time and place to discuss the problem.

Step 2: Describe the situation or issue clearly in a way that is agreeable to both of you, such as "We can't agree on the problem" or "Our problem is not knowing what the problem is."

Step 3: Describe how specific behaviors in this situation cause a problem for you, even if it is not a problem for your spouse.

Step 4: Describe your personal reactions to this situation, such as "when we argue I feel afraid that something bad will happen and it scares me."

Step 5: State the outcome result (your objective) that you want to happen.

Step 6: Brainstorm to find possible alternate outcomes, such as "Find a counselor we both like."

Step 7: Agree on a plan, an outcome goal that you both will work to make happen.

Step 8: Try your plan and then review to see how well you accomplished your goal.

A professional therapist may be licensed as a marriage and family counselor or may be a pastoral counselor, psychologist, social worker, psychiatrist, or other professional person. The exact types of licenses vary according to the laws of your state. With your mentor couple, you and your partner can explore your situation more thoroughly and then implement the solution that you choose.

EXPLORE 2.3G: Seeking Professional Help

How do you know when you need professional help? If you are clear about the general type of assistance you need, seek a competent professional person in that field. If you are not sure, consult with a support couple or your minister. Some sources for help are listed in the resources at the end of this book.

You know you need professional help when . . .

• the attempt to solve problems produces more problems and frustrations than solutions.

• you feel just as bad when the solution works as when it does not.

• you never seem to find time to talk about problems.

• one or both of you refuse to work on problems.

• most changes in your behavior are worse, not better.

• you are certain you are OK; it is your partner who needs help.

• you continue to feel depressed, no matter what your partner does or does not do.

• you lose control of yourself in some situations.

• you hate to go home, or you wish your partner would not come home.

• fewer and fewer things seem to make sense.

• you suspect your partner or others of wanting to harm you whenever they get the chance.

• most things seem to be beyond your control.

• you feel guilty about most things, or you often feel you are a complete failure.

• you can't define the problem and talking about problems only makes them worse.

If you answered yes to more than two or three of these statements, you and your partner should talk with a trained coach, support couple, pastor, or professional therapist..

2.4

POSITIVES: SATISFACTION, GROWTH

Celebrations, milestones, and markers along your lifetime marriage journey reaffirm your joy and renew your satisfaction in your marriage. These are your rituals for expressing shared meanings that bind you together as a married couple. You may adapt some rituals from your families of origin or from observing other couples. You may also create unique rituals that emerge out of your special experiences together.

Basic Affirmation and Blessing Rituals

Celebration rituals and other patterns help keep you alive and renew special appreciations. Use this framework to create ways you bless and strengthen each other, based on research by John Gottman.

Blessings at Partings

When you leave each other for work, school, or other daily activities, ask your partner for one thing you will affirm or bless in your partner's day. Give your partner your blessing and remember to think about and pray that your partner can handle that task well or share that joy. The word *good-bye* is actually a contraction of "God be with you." Allow two or three minutes each morning (or whenever you part) for this mutual hug and blessing.

Welcome Celebration at Reuniting

Allow fifteen to twenty minutes each evening (or other close of your work day) first to thank each other for getting back home safely and to listen to each other about the day's events. Don't try to solve problems or complain about being late. Do embrace as though you have been apart for months. Do welcome and affirm each other.

Give Appreciation and Admiration

In addition to the blessings and welcomes, at least once every day tell your spouse a specific way that you appreciate him or her. For example, "I like your smile" or "Thank you for helping me (in a specific way)." If you are away, do this by notes hidden in your home or luggage, and by phone or e-mail.

Exchange Affection

Warmly hold each other, kiss, and touch each other in ways that express your care. Kiss each other goodnight and exchange "I love you" every night (even if you don't feel like it at times). Surround disagreements and stresses with your assurance that you do love and care for each other so nothing will ever be so big that you will allow it to split you apart.

Weekly Date Night

Have at least one evening (or other extended time) when you do something enjoyable together. Don't solve problems. Do assume you are on a special date when you want to impress your partner with how much you care and want to discover her or his dreams, hopes, or special longings.

Adapt these basic patterns of affirmation rituals to your lifestyle. They may not be new if you are already doing them. Keep enjoying these rituals in various ways until they become second nature, then continue doing them because they are fun. It may take forty or fifty years for you to discover the wisdom in these rituals.

Holidays, Celebrations, Symbols

Holidays and celebrations can be times for refreshment and renewing your visions for your future. Such times offer opportunities to reaffirm your relationship with others. These special days can provide the common experiences that help to unify couples, families, and communities.

Holidays

Holidays come from "holy days" and are important reminders of events in our common history, and they can be important for a couple or family activities. Holidays can be a reunion and the sharing of experiences with friends and relatives. Holidays may also be times of increased tension for some couples. Since there is often more time to be together, the opportunity for conflict increases. Some people may feel sad or depressed because of unresolved inner feelings, or because others seem to be so much happier or more successful. Children are usually out of school on holidays, and this may create more stress for some parents.

Celebrations

To celebrate means to honor, to proclaim, to extol, and to sound the praises of someone or of some event. On his or her birthdays, you can honor and praise the life of that person. Through these celebrations, relatives and friends can tell a person how important he or she is to them. Your wedding anniversary is your very special day to renew your commitment and share your appreciation for being with each other.

Worship in your home is also a celebration. In worship, you give "worth-ship" to God in appreciation for the gifts of life and love. You may celebrate God's continuous love to you and to others with a prayer at mealtime; by reading from the Bible and devotional materials; by sharing poems and inspiring thoughts for the day; and through music and other art forms. Having a worship celebration each day can be an opportunity to grow in love and appreciation of each other, of other persons, and of God.

Symbols

Symbols remind us of important persons and groups in our lives. They point to realities beyond themselves. Symbols help us express who we are and what we value. They help us form common bonds with others who share similar views. You and your partner have symbols that are special for you. Pictures, clothing, rings, gifts, and music help recall special events in your lives, which bring you closer together.

Art forms may also remind you of important life dimensions. Music, photographs, paintings, and sculpture help you celebrate your human relationships. Again and again, symbols call you to renew your awareness of the many ways in which God and other persons care for you. Symbols also may remind you to reach out to others with care, concern, love, and encouragement.

EXPLORE 2.4A: Symbols and Meanings

Together, talk about holidays, celebrations, and symbols that have special meanings for you. Here are some possible areas:

1. What is your favorite holiday? In what way is it important to your marriage?
2. Do your holidays involve your relatives or friends? When do job responsibilities prevent you from enjoying some holidays?
3. What did each of your childhood families celebrate? Share some special memories of family celebrations. How do these influence the celebrations you and your partner have?
4. Together, look at pictures or other symbols of your relationship. How do these remind you of past experiences or future goals?
5. Do you have special music that you think of as "our song"? Talk about the words and what the music means for you.
6. What other symbols are important for you?

Your Personal Faith

Your personal faith includes your life philosophy, your perspectives toward life, and your assumptions about yourself and others, which you express in your daily conversation and actions. You may have a formal creed or other statement of faith, but your attitudes and expectations express your personal faith.

Whatever your beliefs, they are based upon your life experiences thus far. Out of those experiences you decide to trust, or not to trust, others and God. Your faith involves your hopes and decisions.

Your faith is your perspective on your relationship with others and with God's creation in the universe and in earth. If you assume that the universe is unfriendly and threatening, your faith can be bad or sour. If you experience the world and other persons as being friendly and supportive to you, your faith becomes trust and confidence.

Your personal faith development is mixed into your marriage journey. The mystery and communion of marriage can enable you to understand God as you understand each other

Faith Stages

Your personal faith begins in infancy and continues to develop across your life. Each stage builds on previous experiences. Your faith began with models for ways to live that you saw in the persons who cared for you and in stories of good and bad. On this basis specific instructions about right and wrong gave you many commandments that guide your attitudes and actions.

By adolescence you increasingly evaluated the models and instructions you experienced as you search for and create your own faith for living, your code of conduct. As an adult you reflect on your models, rules, and questions to revise and recombine these in more satisfying ways that address adult levels of cooperation, sexuality, religion, money, and honesty.

As you journey through adulthood and marriage, you face new challenges to the principles you consider most valid. Faith becomes more interpersonal and a matter of inward commitment, the heart and soul of life. God's love gives grace, security, and flexibility to continue to grow in love. Your own security enables you to be open to others without losing your own principles and commitments.

God's primary purpose in marriage and family relationships is to enable us to learn to love more completely and practice care with each other in our homes. Home relationships grow out of your faith, your soul's home, where you learn to give grace as well as receive it.

EXPLORE 2.4B: Personal Faith Experiences

In this exercise, it is important that you listen with respect as your partner describes his or her experience. Encourage each other in sharing, yet be careful not to push your partner to share more than she or he wishes to express.

These questions may help you to explore your peak experiences:

1. What peak experiences have you had? When? How often? Where? What made these experiences so special for you? In what ways have these special times helped you to understand and appreciate yourself, your partner, others, the universe, and/or God?
2. What sense of mystery, amazement, or ecstasy accompanied your experience? Do these feelings continue now? How have these changed you?
3. What basic beliefs do you each have? How do you apply them?
4. On which facets of your personal faiths do you and your partner agree? Where do you disagree? How do you use these beliefs to grow in your understanding of each other and of life?
5. For what do you give praise to God through prayers of thanks? For what do you ask through prayers of petition? Try making lists of your praises and prayers and then compare your lists together.

Prayer and Praise

Prayer is conversation with God, talking with and listening to God. In talking with God we give praise for our many blessings and gifts and ask God's presence in our daily lives. These are signs of God's love and grace to us. Through prayer we express our concerns for other persons and for ourselves.

Prayer includes all the colors of the rainbow. Prayer includes praise, thanksgiving, confession, acknowledgment, affirmation, emotions, thinking, inspiration, contemplation, silence, wrestling, requests, cries of pain and anguish, laughter, and more through all the shades of human experience and communication. Prayer may be individual or group, voiced or silent. Prayers may be prepared or spontaneous, with words or emotional sighs, in fancy words or just plain talk.

Prayer as request or pleading is asking God for beneficial changes in our lives and the lives of others and for other divine interventions. Since we ultimately ask for God's will to be done, our prayers may be for understanding of how our concerns fit into the larger picture of God's purposes and concerns for all persons and the earth. We ask for guidance as we seek to do God's will and share love with others.

Prayer is also listening to God. Listening includes meditation and worship where we listen for God's voice and presence through music, arts, silence, and other channels. Stained glass windows, altars, pictures, reading Scripture and hymns, and nature also enhance worship settings.

In congregational worship each step offers opportunity to discern how God is speaking to us through the Scriptures, hymns, affirmations, sermons, and prayers of confession and commitment. Listening also involves discerning when God is speaking a truth to us through our conversations and experiences with spouse, family members, friends, and strangers.

Uniting together in the Lord's Prayer and other prayers brings a sense of unity and support. The voices of others speak to our spirits, just as joining our voice to others affirms them also.

Realizing you are in the presence of God is the beginning of prayer. God's presence may be obvious, as in the beauties of nature, the joys of life, and the laughter of children. God may be hidden as when we feel alone or lost. At times God may withdraw to give us room to grow, like a caring parent who without interfering watches children at play, yet ready to intervene when the situation becomes dangerous or beyond their abilities.

Special Growth Experiences

Some personal experiences are so compelling and impressive that people will rearrange their life perspectives around them. These peak experiences are like being on a mountain and receiving a direct contact with God. Often these special experiences provide a broader viewpoint from which to interpret life and marriage and to understand God's work with us. It may be difficult to describe your special peak experiences. Symbols, stories, and songs may

---

EXPLORE 2.4C

Use the following to begin your list of thanksgiving, praise, and prayer requests and growth. As you complete the following consider events, qualities, habits, and relationships.

I give thanks to God for _____

I praise God for God's _____

I pray for guidance concerning _____

My prayer concerns are _____

Requests or searchings to lift to God _____

Compare your lists with each other. Take time now to pray with God, both silently and aloud, about these elements. Make this a daily habit in your home.

help label intense feelings, but some experiences are beyond words. For some persons, spiritual and religious terms can be used to describe these very personal encounters; other persons may use scientific, artistic, or mystical terminology.

Some Postwedding Adjustments

How does it feel to be a married couple? Couples face many adjustments during the first months or years of their marriage. If you are not yet married, try to predict how you would react. If you are now married, consider how you are handling these issues.

Your Name

The traditional assumption in some cultures has been the wife assumes her husband's name. For many couples, this is no longer the case. Some choose to call themselves by the husband's last name, some by a combination of both last names, some by the wife's name, and some choose a name different from either family name. Your new name may be from another time, another language, or it may signify some experience you have had. Whatever your choice, your name is the expression of your mutual identity and carries great emotional investment.

Your Residence

Getting married usually means that one or both partners move to a new residence. Selecting a place to live can be difficult as you consider the advantages and disadvantages of various locations. The many details to be considered can produce fatigue and stress that will probably affect your relationship. If both partners move to a new residence, then each of you can feel that the residence really is "ours" from the beginning. The many decisions needed to make it "feel like home" probably will be made jointly.

Memories

Your wedding is a major milestone in the life that you share together. Remembering your wedding encourages you to renew your hopes and aspirations and keep your marriage alive. How will (or do) you preserve the pictures and other reminders of your wedding in ways that keeps your marriage growing?

In addition to saving photographs, tape recordings, and other remembrances, some couples freeze some of their wedding cake. On their first anniversary, they remember their wedding as they enjoy the cake and continue to strive toward their goals, make plans, and share dreams.

Roles and Responsibilities

Many persons have difficulty believing that they really are free to create their own lifestyle in ways that are unique for them. The effort to make your marriage fit the patterns of your parents, relatives, or friends can cause many problems. The statement, "My family never did it that way" is sure to complicate your marriage. Working together, you and your partner can establish your own responsibilities and modify your roles as seems best for both of you. Reading and talking with other couples enlarges the range of models you can choose.

Few persons like to wash dishes, clean bathrooms, or carry out garbage, yet these and other menial jobs are part of housekeeping, whether you are married or single. Together, you can consider all the details of homemaking and agree to share the unpleasant as well as the pleasant responsibilities. There are no tasks, duties, or roles that are automatically "supposed to be" done by the wife or by the husband. As spouses, you each agree to assume responsibilities according to your skills and interests.

As you gain experience, you probably will need to revise the roles that you established initially. Allow maintenance times when you can talk over your views about the way you have organized your responsibilities. When conflicts occur, you can use your communication and problem-solving skills to improve your patterns.

Physical Challenges

Some couples may need to adjust to the physical challenges of one or both partners. Chronic conditions, such as a dysfunctional body organ or restrictions on the ability to walk, talk, or participate in activities, may be a continuing challenge in your marriage. Even if you and your partner have no major physical challenges, you may need to consider these factors in activities with others.

Energy and Activity Levels

Some days or times during the day you are probably more aware and active than others. You each have several cycles of physical and psychological functioning that are influenced by your body and by events around you. Shifts in your mood and energy levels can underlie some of the ups and downs in your relationship. Personal rhythms are unique for each of you but they are not as fixed as some would have you believe. When these cycles fit together, you will respond in a different manner than in those periods when you are at opposite ends of your cycles. Energy levels are also related to jobs, sleep, food intake, and general health.

Stimulation and Quietness

You each may want different types of stimulation at various times. One may enjoy a loud radio, much television, and more noise, excitement, and activity than the other likes. At some times, each of you may want more physical contact, hugging, and caressing than usual. One of you may prefer more quiet and solitude, and activities such as reading or crafts. As you each seek the type of stimulation you prefer, also consider your partner's desires.

Wakefulness and Sleep

Different people require different amounts of sleep in order to feel well rested. If one partner needs more sleep, the other can consider this in arranging his or her waking time. A partner may be an early riser, a day person, or a night owl. You may need to coordinate your sexual activities with your energy and sleep cycles.

Activity Patterns

Some persons always prefer to be on the go, while others would rather relax at home with hobbies or other quiet activities. If you and your partner have similar activity patterns, fewer disagreements will arise. As you develop your own patterns, the important common element is that you agree on the patterns.

EXPLORE 2.4D: Lifestyle and Hope

Plan some talk time, and together, review the various issues mentioned in this chapter. Decide which of these, or other issues, you will explore. Here are some guides:

1. Consider the sound of "Mr. and Mrs. _____" in contrast to "Mrs. and Mr. _____." Does the order of your names make any difference to you? How does your name or the combination of names express the way you see your marriage and yourselves?

2. How long will you be in your current residence? How do you feel about moving? What moving or household arrangement differences have you had? How do you resolve these?

3. How do (or will) you preserve and use your wedding and other memories?

4. How have you assigned homemaking responsibilities? What changes would you like to make now? What do you think, feel, and want concerning these?

5. Which partner enjoys more stimulation? Who would rather talk? listen? How do you cope with loss of energy, fatigue, or sickness? What happens when one partner's cycles seem to interfere with the other's rhythms or desires?

6. What physical or skill challenges affect your marriage? How do you cope with these?

Theme Three

Love as Daily Caring

EXPRESSIONS of LOVE

Let love be genuine, hold fast to what is good.
Love one another with healthy family affection;
outdo one another in showing honor to each other.
Never drop our zeal; be aglow with the Spirit.
Rejoice in our hope; be patient in difficulties.
Love does no wrong to a spouse.
The commandments for marriage are summed up in this sentence:
You shall love your spouse as yourself. (paraphrase from Romans 12:8-21)

Beloved, since God so loved us, we ought to love one another.
No one has ever seen God; if we love one another,
God lives in us, and his love is perfected in us.
By this we know that we abide in him and he in us,
because he has given us of his Spirit. (1 John 4:11-13, NRSV)

Pastor to the woman:
Name, *will you have* Name *to be your husband, to live together in holy marriage? Will you love him, comfort him, honor and keep him, in sickness and in health, and forsaking all others, be faithful to him as long as you both shall live?*

Pastor to the man:
Name, *will you have* Name *to be your wife, to live together in holy marriage? Will you love her, comfort her, honor and keep her, in sickness and in health, and forsaking all others, be faithful to her as long as you both shall live?*
> —*from the "Service of Christian Marriage,"* The United Methodist Hymnal, *pages 864-69*

EXPLORE 3: What Do *You* Mean by Love?

Love has many meanings. In the following list, circle the words and phrases that best describe love for you. Then discuss your choices. An alternate choice is to make a set of love-word cards. Put one word on each card. Let one of you draw a card and either you or your partner make a sentence using that word to express your love to the other.

care	concern	sacrifice	sensitive
warmth	dependable	excited	affection
independent	forgiving	obey	putting others first
cooperation	hugs, kisses	choice	accepting
attitude	remembering	changeless	keeping promises
sharing	surprises	_____	_____

Try using some love words in sentences with your partner. You may write your statements or give them orally. What new expression of love will you give to your partner next time you see her or him?

3.1

HOME, LIFESTYLE, HEALTH

Give us this day our daily bread. And forgive us our debts, as we also have forgiven our debtors. And do not bring us to the time of trial, but rescue us from the evil one. (Matthew 6:11-13, NRSV)

The resources, skills, and attitudes you have explored in the themes of faith and power are involved in all areas of your marriage. With your increased awareness of your covenant, expectations, backgrounds, process of communication, and problem solving, in this third theme of love we focus on three specific relationships in marriage: couple, family, and work. These are the basic relationships through which you express love. The overall goal of marriage is learning to love. "I love you" has very special meanings for spouses.

What Is Love to You? Many Meanings of Love

Your answer probably involves some type of family relationship. It may be a parent who cared for her or his child, or a family member who fought in a war to protect our freedom and make the world safer for peace. Your image of love may be the quick action of a brother or sister who saved your life, or the strength and warmth of a husband and wife who cared for each other across many years without counting the costs. The enduring support of a friend may also form your image of love.

Expressions of Love

Think of one or two outstanding experiences when you felt truly loved. Suppose you are a reporter trying to understand how these experiences express the meaning of love. Describe one of your special experiences to your partner. When and where did it happen? What was done? What made it special? Why? How do you feel about this now? How can you show love

to your partner? to others? Now, think of one or two special love experiences that you have had with your partner. Separately describe one of these times and then together share your descriptions with each other.

Your Home

A home is more than a house, apartment, or condo. More than just a place to eat, sleep, and store your belongings, your home also reflects your lifestyle, interests, and values. It is an extension of you. Damage to your residence by fire or theft is threatening because of its financial cost and your emotional investments. Your home has at least two levels of meaning for you and your partner.

First, it's functional and practical. Most items in your residence have a specific use. Chairs are for sitting and a refrigerator is for storing food. Your residence and furnishings also have emotional value for you. For instance, some pictures carry meanings and memories of persons important to you. The quality and style of furnishings, books, and other possessions may involve your feelings of self-worth. A certain furniture arrangement may be a matter of "getting your way," as much as for convenience.

Some Stewardship Concerns

Our Christian commitment challenges us, as couples, not only to consider our own needs, resources, talents, and careers, but also to relate to others in God's world. Our Christian stewardship leads us to think about community, national, and world issues as we plan our family budgets and make decisions related to our vocations, possessions, and money.

Considering your home and property involves having a will and may require legal assistance. Every married couple should have an up-to-date will with terms that are agreeable to both partners. A will can avoid complicated probate court procedures in the event of the death of one partner. It may include many matters, such as guardianship of children, provision for care of family, tax implications, trusts, disability income, insurance, pensions, and property. In the case of a couple, a will usually names the surviving spouse as executor. You need to consult with an attorney about details of your will.

Some partners may have property they would like to continue as legally separate after entering marriage. If you wish to maintain any possessions as legally belonging only to one partner, you will need to consult an attorney about details.

EXPLORE 3:1A: Living Space

Allow time together to share your ideas and feelings about your residence and possessions. If possible, go to a residence you have had, now have, or will have, as a couple.

1. Consider your current or recent residential situation (room, apartment, house, or other). What three things did you like best? What were three disadvantages? Describe these.

2. Talk about the residential situation you will have, or hope to have.
   a. In which room will you probably spend most time? Least time?
   b. Who will be responsible for keeping each area clean and in order? How will the other partner help?
   c. How much closet, drawer, and storage space do you each need?
   d. Which area do you value most? least? Describe your reasons.
   e. Do you need to plan space for children who will be living with you and/or those you plan to have?
   f. Will you be living with your parents or other relatives? Will any of them be living in your home?

3. What special hobbies, activities, and interests do you have that will require space in your home? How will you decide on this?

4. What other property, such as automobiles, bicycles, hobby equipment, children's toys, and other items do you have that will require storage? How will you arrange for these?

5. Will you rent, lease, or buy your residence? What issues are involved in this decision?

6. How do you feel about moving to a new residence? How will you locate stores, professional services, new friends, and a church? What makes a residence feel like home to you?

7. Which jobs will each partner do to keep your residence clean, in good repair, and livable? If necessary, could either of you do any job around your residence, including cooking, washing dishes, fixing things, and cleaning?

8. How will you share in these decisions? What feelings do you each have as you think together about your residence? Talk more about these.

3.2

FINANCES, STEWARDSHIP

It's not what you would do if millions should be your lot,
It's what you are doing now with the fifteen dollars you've got!

The way you use your time, money, and belongings reveals your priorities. Although the grammar in the above rhyme could be improved, it emphasizes that money and possessions are linked together in practical and emotional ways for each person.

Money allows us to trade our work and resources for the work and resources of others. Your belongings are the accumulation of this process. In these ways you and your partner express your covenant with each other and your stewardship of your part of God's Creation.

Meanings of Money

A person who sows sparingly will also reap sparingly, and one who sows bountifully will also reap bountifully. You must do as you have decided, not reluctantly or under compulsion, for God loves a cheerful giver (2 Corinthians 9:7).

Money itself is not the root of problems, but the value you place on money and possessions may cause difficulties (1 Timothy 6:10). Money elicits your personal feelings about getting what you want, sharing limited resources, and compromising on priorities. Money and possessions may bring problems, as well as opportunities for growth, because it usually forces decisions about your relationship as a couple. When the amount of available money is limited, you may be able to carry out only some of the activities you have planned.

Money has potential symbolic meanings. Money conflicts are often about freedom, power, independence, love, security, competence, achievement, and acceptance. Gridlock conflicts about budgets, expenses, investments, or other money matters carry hidden meanings, such as feeling frustrated or blocked from reaching a dream. Exploring these underlying feelings helps you get out of gridlock and frees you to find practical solutions.

Two Major Money Decisions

The handling of your money involves two major functions: the executive-decision tasks and the secretary-treasurer tasks.

Mutual trust is basic to good money management. You can arrange your spending in many different ways. Maintaining good credit relieves anxiety and shows your responsibility as a couple. Your handling of finances can enhance your relationship, or it can strain and perhaps destroy it. If one spouse tries to hold the purse strings too tight, it often causes the other spouse to slip around to buy things they want and try to hide it as groceries or some other category that seems acceptable.

In the executive-decision tasks, you and your partner need to agree on the way you will make decisions concerning the use of your money. You may determine that in certain categories, one of you will implement the decisions, as with buying groceries or gasoline. In other purchases, such as home furnishings or a car, you may decide that both partners will be fully involved.

The roles called the secretary-treasurer tasks include balancing your checkbook, paying bills, writing checks, and keeping good records of income and expenditures. In deciding which partner will do each of these, you will need to consider which of you has more time, skill, and interest. It can be either husband or wife, providing you agree on the general procedure.

Be clear in separating the secretary-treasurer from the executive-decision functions. Sometimes it is easy to assume the person who signs the credit card slip or writes the checks automatically has final say over the way money is spent. Prompt payment of obligations and record-keeping require the desire and cooperation of both partners. This helps to eliminate many arguments over where the money has gone.

Some Special Money Situations

Two Incomes

If both partners are employed, how much of both incomes is needed for your basic expenses? It is important to talk about alternate plans in case of pregnancy, serious disease, or disabling injury. Layoffs or changes in the economy may cause an unexpected loss of income. What are your backup and savings plans for these contingencies?

One Breadwinner

If you plan for only one spouse to earn all the income, how does this earner feel about the other spouse not working? Is one working to put the other spouse through school, or so the other spouse can care for children, or other goals?

New to Living on Your Own

If you never have experienced living on your own income, you and your partner might take the amount set aside for food on your spending plan in the "Explore" exercise, and go to a supermarket or other store to price items you would need for two weeks of meals. You might shop for a major home appliance and compare the costs of paying cash with buying on credit.

From Individual to Couple

If you have been accustomed to living on your own income, how will you now combine your money lifestyle with your partner's money lifestyle?

Credit and Debts

For some couples, credit installment payments and unpaid debts are problems. Some persons may be impulse buyers, or they may have prewedding debts to pay after the wedding. It is essential to be honest about debts, loans, and other financial obligations that may become part of your marriage. Feelings about these matters need to be discussed openly.

Children

If you have children or plan to have children, what are the options you might have for working after children are born? Some couples with children decide both partners will work part-time, so each can share in the parenting. In many cases, both partners continue in their full-time jobs by using the services of a trusted, competent person or agency for child care.

EXPLORE 3.2A: Money and Power

Money represents power, and decisions about money involve shifts in the amount of power or control that each of you has in your relationship. These power issues also may appear in decisions about your residential space and material things. Talk about conflicts you have concerning money.

Is the person who earns the money the one who decides how to spend it?
Which expenditures do you feel are more controlled by your partner than you want? How do you want to change this pattern?
What worries or fears do you have concerning money?
Which of you is a saver/spender? How are these patterns related to your sense of self-worth? Your past experiences?
How much interest do your credit card debt, mortgage, and other loans cost you per month? In what ways is this a problem? What are your plans tor paying off these debts? Would it be fair to declare bankruptcy?
What is first in your life? How does your use of money show your values and priorities in life? What other money issues do you face now?

Obligations from Previous Marriages, Child Support, or Family Responsibilities

Child Support Obligations

If you must make child-support payments, what budget adjustments need to be made in your current budget? How does your spouse feel about the financial and parenting responsibilities you bring to your current marriage?

Alimony

If you have financial obligations to a previous partner, what proportion of your current income does this require? In what ways does this continuing involvement with a past relationship affect your current finances and lifestyle?

Family Obligations

Any previous financial obligations to your parents or other relatives affect availability of money in your present marriage. Is either partner financially responsible for parents or other relatives due to their aging, health, or chronic condition? In what ways are these shared with your siblings, if any? Are these permanent because the parent or relative will never be able to be self-supporting? Are these temporary, such as a loan to be paid or gifts to help on medical expenses or home expenses? Plans and feelings about these obligations need to be discussed. Even if you are not involved now in these obligations, you and your partner might talk over your feelings and ideas about parents or other relatives who may become your financial responsibility in the future.

On Giving Money Away

One way to express your appreciation for the blessings you receive through work and money is to share these resources. We encourage you to set aside a specific percentage of your income (a tithe) to help others. Many couples set a proportion of their total income (such as 10 percent) for the church and for community and world needs. We hope this will be your lifelong pattern of generous sharing. For this reason it is placed near the top of the budget outline that follows. Giving to others is so important in helping couples regard the use of all their income as a stewardship of God's resources.

Plan Times to Review Issues

Income, expenditures, and other financial matters change during a marriage. It is important to have times when you and your partner can discuss comfortably all money and income issues. You also can find information and assistance in books, personal finance seminars, and from banks, insurance, and home finance companies. Financial opinions and advice vary widely, and you need to evaluate all information from the viewpoint of Christian stewardship in your marriage.

It helps to have a regular time each week or month to discuss the details of your income and spending. This also can be a time to renew goals and discuss longer-range expenditures and larger purchases. There are many variations in the way you blend your work, money, and marriage, so continue to be open and grow as you discuss and negotiate priorities. Your marriage is unique, so the ways you handle money and possessions reflect your special situation. Adapt what you learn from others to your situation.

In your marriage, will you (or do you) have a joint checking account, separate accounts, and/or credit cards? Will you pool your incomes, or keep them identifiably separate? How do you feel about your method of paying for purchases? Are there times when either of you tries to use money to control your partner? Which of the secretary-treasurer tasks will each of you do?

After you have talked about your money-management functions, plan additional time to set up your income and spending plan. Whether you call this a budget, a plan, or something else, it still means you and your partner are the ones who decide how much money will be set aside for each category.

EXPLORE 3.2B Managing Your Money

Explore your basic plans for managing your money. Allow plenty of time to discuss your "executive-decision tasks" first. Which items are mutual decisions, and which does each partner make separately? How do you both feel about your decision patterns?

You may make your entries independently and then combine them in this chart, or you can each place a figure on the line as you talk together about each category. With either procedure, be alert to your feelings as you arrive at your figures.

Begin by assuming a realistic amount for your income for the next twelve months. If your income varies during the year, finding your monthly average can help you plan to hold extra income from the higher months to use in the low-income months. You may prefer to subtract your taxes and Social Security payments to arrive at your basic available income.

Our Annual Income:
$_____ from wife's work, career, job
$_____ from husband's work, career, job
$_____ from other sources
$_____ Total Annual Income

Divide the total by 12 to find
    your Monthly Average Income: $_____

Less Taxes and Social Security: $_____
Monthly Take-Home Income: $_____

Your Spending Plan:	Initial HUSBAND	Initial WIFE	Adjusted Amount	Actual Amounts
contributions: church, others	_____	_____	_____	_____
taxes and Social Security	_____	_____	_____	_____
saving, emergencies	_____	_____	_____	_____
health, life insurance	_____	_____	_____	_____
housing, utilities	_____	_____	_____	_____
food (including eating out)	_____	_____	_____	_____
clothing	_____	_____	_____	_____
personal money for wife	_____	_____	_____	_____
personal money tor husband	_____	_____	_____	_____
transportation expenses	_____	_____	_____	_____
job-related expenses	_____	_____	_____	_____
education	_____	_____	_____	_____
payments for purchases on credit	_____	_____	_____	_____
leisure and recreation	_____	_____	_____	_____
child support	_____	_____	_____	_____
caring for parents/relatives	_____	_____	_____	_____
other obligations	_____	_____	_____	_____
other expenditures	_____	_____	_____	_____
TOTALS $	_____	_____	_____	_____

Take time to talk about balancing your expenditures and income. Share together the way you feel about details of your money management.
Taxes and Social Security were included in the list as a reminder of the part of your income that goes for those purposes.

3.3

SEXUALITY, AFFECTION, NURTURE

There are many ways to love . . .
and sex is one of them.
There are many sexual expressions of love. . .
and sexual intercourse is one of them.

You nurture and care for each other in many ways. Through your sexual activities, you express your tenderness, care, and love for each other. Words of endearment, touches, smiles, and hugs are only a few of the expressions of your sexual love.

As with other ways of communicating, sexual activities have a great deal of potential for providing shared meanings between partners. Occasions of physical and emotional closeness enable you to renew and deepen the love and grace that God offers you as a sexual being.

Sexuality is more than nudity and genital contact between partners. Sexuality, as used here, includes all the ways that you express yourself through your gender as female or male. This is your personality. God has created you so your thoughts, expectations, feelings, and wishes can become known to your partner through the erotic possibilities your body provides. Depending upon the way you feel about yourself and about your partner, your sexual behaviors can greatly enrich your intimacies as a couple.

Knowing Each Other

It is significant that the Bible uses the verb "to know" to describe sexual relations between a man and a woman. As you and your partner consider your feelings and wants concerning money, possessions, careers, children, and other areas, you experience greater intimacy and closeness.

Emotional closeness usually is expressed by being physically close enough to talk and to touch. This physical closeness makes your feelings, positive and negative, more intense, partly because physical contact can bring either pain or pleasure.

Your sexual intimacy is an important part of your covenant as partners. Through your sexual relationship, you come to know each other more completely, and your unconditional acceptance of each other can become very real and beautiful.

Through sexual activity, your language of love inspires new creative forms, techniques, and approaches. Together, your sexual communication can be a growing crescendo of love as you freely and fully give yourselves to each other, with the deeper meanings of sexual love becoming most genuine through your long-term relationship.

More Than Information

Accurate information about sexuality and sexual functioning is necessary for a happy and fulfilling relationship. However, your attitudes of warmth, respect, and tenderness with each other in lovemaking are more important than sexual techniques and information. You can learn together and blend your skills into your own symphony of enjoyment. Like music and other forms of art, your sexual relationship depends upon the use of your mastery of basics to create more messages of love between your partner and yourself.

Some Basic Assumptions

Here are some Christian perspectives that express views about sexuality. As you read them, consider your own feelings and beliefs about your sexuality as a couple.

Your personality is expressed in physical and spiritual dimensions. No action is only physical or only spiritual. Your personality and spirit are blended with body and brain to shape your thoughts into the words you speak. Like all life, sex is both physical and spiritual—flesh and spirit. Since sexual behavior has spiritual, emotional, intentional, and physical dimensions, you are not merely a sex organ, but a whole person. God has created you so that you can express yourself through your sexuality. Thus physical sex alone becomes an idol. God has created sex to be part of your whole lives together.

In the Bible and in current Christian thinking, human sexuality is clearly affirmed for its creative possibilities between partners. In the Old Testament, the Song of Solomon describes a wide range of sexual feelings as expressions of love between a man and a woman.

How fair and pleasant you are,
*   O loved one, delectable maiden!*
You are stately as a palm tree,
*   and your breasts are like its clusters. . . .*

I am my beloved's,
*   and his desire is for me.*

Come, my beloved,
*   let us go forth into the fields . . .*

There I will give you my love . . . .

The voice of my beloved
*   Look he comes . . . .*
Let me see your face,
*   for your voice is sweet,*
*   and your face lovely.*
*   (Song of Solomon, 7:6-7, 10, 11; 2:8, 14, NRSV)*

With or without intercourse, sexual activities are affirmed by God and by the church today as a major way in which married partners can share love and tenderness and enrich each other as persons.

Women and men are equal before God in their participation in sexual expressions of love. Today some may consider the apostle Paul's comments about sexuality to be limited. However, in the context of New Testament life, his comments about married love were very advanced. In 1 Corinthians 7, Paul assumed a couple would have a full range of sexual relationships that could be initiated by either spouse. "Do not cheat each other of normal sexual intercourse, unless of course you both decide to abstain temporarily to make special opportunity for prayer. But afterwards you should resume relations as before" (1 Corinthians. 7:5, JBP).

On the basis of your covenant, as partners you choose together how you will express affection toward each other. It is important for both spouses that sexual preferences and concerns be discussed. When additional information is needed about any area of sexual functioning, you can seek help together.

Sexual intercourse is for pleasure and procreation. Planning for the conception, birth, and parenting of children is the responsibility of husband and wife. To assume this responsibility, both partners need accurate information about contraceptives in order to find a method for regular use that both prefer. Each child should be wanted and planned.

Your response to God's covenant of love is the root of your understandings and agreements concerning sexual activities. Fidelity and faithfulness between partners refers to all areas of marriage, not just to sexual concerns. Faithfulness suggests you

EXPLORE 3.3A: Sexuality

For this exercise, you will need magazines that contain pictures of adults of various ages.

With your partner, select several pictures you consider to be most expressive of the way you understand sexuality and intimacy between a man and a woman. Describe the way each picture shows this.

Look also at other pictures that present distorted or misleading views of human sexuality. Give details for your reasons. Pictures may be from stories, advertisements, cartoons, or other sources.

Separately, write several sentences that describe the way you understand sexuality in your relationship. Give specific examples of behaviors that are important to you. Talk together about your statements. Touch or hold each other as you talk.

and your partner can depend upon each other's love and care at all times. To be present, open, and concerned about each other expresses faithfulness and dependability between partners.

The Sexual Response Cycle

The human sexual-response cycle during intercourse is usually described as consisting of four major phases, each gradually progressing to the next level.

Arousal and Excitement begin as tender caresses, strokes, kisses, and other foreplay activities that increase sexual interest and prepare for intercourse. Perfume, music, and romantic talk add variety. These expressions of love are enjoyable in themselves and are essential for adequate vaginal lubrication and for penile erection.

Plateau or Leveling continues for an extended time as partners continue to stimulate each other in mutually pleasurable ways.

Climax occurs with a varied pattern of intense muscular contractions in both partners, including ejaculation by the male. The intensity, number, length, and pattern of orgasm in each partner depends upon energy levels, health, feelings, and attitudes.

Resolution and Relaxation brings a gradual return to the sexually unaroused level. The fullness of personal sharing during this extended period of time can promote special closeness, unity, and renewal of appreciation between partners, bringing them together as more complete persons who know more of the mystery of each other.

Patterns Are Different

The sequence of excitement, plateau, orgasm, and resolution may or may not include coitus (penile-vaginal intercourse). Usually insertion of the penis into the vagina is part of the sequence, but the sexual-response cycle also may occur in relation to noncoital stimulation between partners.

On some occasions partners may return to earlier excitement and additional orgasm experiences after relaxation and rest. Your patterns, levels, duration, intensities, and enjoyment of each stage will vary on different occasions of sexual activity; perhaps no two occasions will be identical. Sexual interest, desire, and energy vary in each partner at different times and under different conditions. General health, fatigue, stress and tension, conflicts, menstruation, time schedules, moods, use of alcohol or other drugs, and other factors influence each partner's sensitivity. Some occasions of sexual activity end in disappointment or frustration for every couple. From these, partners learn to appreciate and accept each other in ways that can remove the pressure to perform perfectly in sexual areas.

At times sexual intercourse and pleasuring will produce extreme ecstasy and a tremendous sense of oneness and mutual satisfaction. On other occasions they will be very comfortable and satisfying, without being prolonged or unusual. No one outcome is "correct" but every pattern and experience can be an opportunity to love and affirm each other through sexual relations.

Sexual Difficulties

Some sexual difficulties occasionally occur for couples. Many times the difficulty will disappear if the partners do not become upset, anxious, demanding,

---

EXPLORE 3.3B: Sexual Pleasuring

Talking about sexual preferences and behaviors may be more difficult than performing them. Allow some uninterrupted private time together to share your feelings about discussing sexual matters. You might begin by completing this sentence: "When I talk about sex, I feel . . ."

When you become more comfortable, consider some of the sexual activities you enjoy, or would enjoy. Describe the behavior, tell what it means to you, and talk about how you feel. What expectations about sexual intimacy do each of you bring to your marriage? Which behaviors do you dislike? At which times do you feel rejected or most loved by what your partner wants or does?

or preoccupied with the problem. Incorrect or limited information about sexual functioning may cause problems for partners. Partners often can increase their sexual satisfaction by obtaining good sexual information and training. Some resources listed in this book can provide additional information.

There are several common sexual dysfunctions that typically have psychological causes:

Males

Erectile dysfunction—inability to achieve and/or maintain erection sufficient to complete coitus, on an average of at least three-fourths of the occasions of intercourse.

Premature ejaculation—ejaculation occurs too soon, usually within less than a minute after entry into the vagina.

Ejaculatory incompetence—inability to ejaculate inside the vagina, but ejaculation may result from masturbation.

Females

Orgasmic dysfunction—either never has had an orgasm or has had orgasms previously but not at present.

Dyspareunia—painful intercourse, even with sufficient foreplay and vaginal lubrication.

Vaginismus—powerful, painful involuntary contraction of vaginal muscles that prevent entry of penis.

If a sexual difficulty or dysfunction continues to prevent satisfactory sexual relations, seek appropriate professional assistance. Your minister or physician can help you to clarify the issues and locate well-qualified professional persons as needed.

Some techniques for overcoming sexual challenges are simple to use. If one spouse wants more sexual activity than the other partner enjoys, seek compromises that still express your love for each other.

Sexual difficulties often reflect stresses in other areas of the partners' relationship. Exploring the attitudes, preferences, self-images, expectations, and other factors presented in this guide also may help partners to more enjoyable sexual relations. Your covenant of unconditional love becomes especially important in this area.

Contraception

There are several methods to control conception in the event a couple does not wish to conceive a child. These are listed under three headings below. You may obtain more details from the resources listed in this book, and your minister, counselor, or physician also can assist you. Some community agencies, such as Planned Parenthood and city or county health departments, provide inexpensive assistance with contraceptives.

Unreliable Methods

These contraceptive methods are not dependable:

Douche—This is not necessary and often not recommended for feminine cleanliness. The douche cannot reach sperm that have entered the uterus.

Rhythm—Most women do not know the precise time of their ovulation until after it occurs—too late for contraceptive action.

Withdrawal—Concentrated quantities of semen often are contained in the fluid that discharges from the penis prior to ejaculation, and as a result, semen may be deposited in the vagina before ejaculation occurs.

Fairly Reliable Methods

These methods, if carefully used before intercourse, provide reasonably good contraception without a physician's prescription:

Condom—This must be of good quality and placed on the penis before it is inserted in the vagina. It is the only contraceptive that also protects against sexually transmitted diseases.

Contraceptive cream, jelly, or foam—These can be effective, if carefully and properly inserted in the vagina early enough before intercourse.

Contraceptive cream and condom—Although considered more troublesome, this combination provides more reliable contraceptive protection than condom or cream alone.

Prescription Methods

These methods are usually the most reliable, and they require a physician's prescription or other assistance:

Oral contraceptives—The pill is safe and reliable only if used under the supervision of a physician. Some women have side effects from certain types of contraceptive medications. Some physicians advise being off the pill occasionally in order to check on body rhythms.

Contraceptive patches and related methods—Several newer methods involve a patch, implant, or injection of hormonal chemicals that inhibit the conception cycle.

Diaphragm and contraceptive jelly or cream—The diaphragm must be fitted for the woman by a physician. It should be reinserted correctly into the vagina prior to each intercourse. These methods do not involve an internal chemical change in the woman's body.

Sterilization surgical procedures—vasectomy and usually tubal ligation. These methods are considered permanent, but not absolutely 100 percent certain. They are done only at a time when a couple plans never to conceive children.

Newer contraceptive methods are currently being tested. To secure more information about them, consult with specialists in your community.

Physical Examinations for Both Partners

It is helpful for each of you to have a physical examination. At that time, you can consult with your physician about any sexual and contraceptive concerns you may have. If you have a physical condition that might affect your participation in sexual activities, or if you have concerns about inheritable genetic factors that might affect any children you conceive, talking with specialists in these areas can give you important information and often relieve you of unnecessary worries.

Success in Sexual Relations

You and your partner are the only judges of your sexual compatibility and success. There is no criterion other than your own views and feelings. If you and your partner both are comfortable and pleased with your sexual behaviors, you are successful. The basic limit in the sexual area, as well as in all other areas, is that behaviors do not cause physical or emotional harm to either partner or to others.

Sex is a matter of your entire mind and spirit, as well as a function of your genitals and the other parts of your body. Expectations, feelings, wants, and meanings are more important than physical factors in determining your sexual satisfaction and happiness.

Couple Sexuality

You and your partner determine your sexual activities as part of your total nurturing relationship as a couple. Often your sexual expressions reflect what is happening in other areas of your marriage. Your pleasurable sexual relationship can increase your appreciation of each other and add to those other areas.

We want to emphasize it is very important that you and your spouse continue to talk openly and frankly with each other about your sexual standards, patterns, concerns, and desires. Sexual matters sometimes are difficult or embarrassing for couples to discuss because so much personal self-worth may be invested in sexuality. However, acknowledging these feelings together can help you to be more comfortable with the beautiful, God-given expressions of your sexual love.

Now For the Symphony

With patience and gentleness, explore your sexuality together, being guided by your own awareness of the activities that are uplifting, enjoyable, and stimulating. Freedom, variety, and pleasant surprises can add to your sexual joy, and this will expand into other areas of your relationship. There will be times when sex is not exciting or ecstatic, but together, you can accept those times and learn from them. Your growth occurs as you come to appreciate your uniqueness and your differences, blending these in your own ways in your artistic creations of your sexual love for each other.

EXPLORE 3.3C: Issues in Sexuality

Take enough uninterrupted time together to talk in depth about the information and issues presented here. Add other topics that are important for you.

1. What do you like, and dislike, about being a woman/man? Can you remember when you first became aware of yourself as a girl/boy? How would you feel if you were the opposite gender?

2. From whom did you receive your sex education? What attitudes developed from these experiences are still with you now?

3. Do you have any physical condition that may affect sexual relations? Discuss with your partner ways you can enjoy sexual nurture in the context of your physical challenges.

4. What emotional or psychological characteristics do you think are more typical of men or of women? Talk about these together.

5. When do you feel most "sexy" and attractive to your partner? When is your partner most sexually attractive to you? When are you most sexually excitable? least excitable or interested in sex? What "turns you on" or "turns you off" sexually? How do your physical and emotional rhythms affect your sexual nurturing?

6. Which five words best describe sexual activities? Separately, write at least five words, including slang terms, to describe sexual activities. Then together compare these. Which words express hostility or control of your partner? Which words emphasize love and thoughtfulness for your partner?

7. Sometimes feelings of affection and appreciation for other persons (of both the same and the opposite sex) may be confused with heterosexual or homosexual tendencies. Some persons may have experienced sexual abuse, rape, or homosexual advances. Talk about your feelings concerning these areas.

8. How do you express your sexuality as a person through your dress, speech, gestures, behaviors, and other ways? Describe some of these and talk about the meanings they have for you both.

9. What type of contraceptive method will, or do, you use in your marriage? Whose decision is this? Do you each feel equally responsible for contraception?

10. Some couples conceive much more easily than others, but usually this cannot be known until a couple attempts to have a child. The safest approach is to assume that you might become pregnant with every intercourse and to use contraceptives accordingly.

    How do you feel about taking contraceptive risks and then finding you are pregnant? Conversely, how do you feel about wanting to conceive children but not being able to do so?

11. What would you do if you have an unwanted pregnancy? How does each of you feel about having an unplanned child? an unwanted child? stopping the pregnancy?

12. If you do not already have children, do you plan to allow yourselves at least a year or two to adjust to each other in marriage before you conceive a child?

13. What concerns do you have about sexually transmitted diseases in relation to your sexual activities together? Are either of you HIV positive, at risk of AIDS or other major sexually transmitted diseases?

3.4

CHILDREN, PARENTING, FAMILIES

See what love the Father has given us, that we should he called children of God; and that is what we are beloved, we are God's children now; . . . What we do know is this: when he is revealed we will be like him, for we will see him as he is.   *(1 John 3:1-2, NRSV)*

We are sometimes childlike, sometimes childish, but always we are God's children.

Alternatives Concerning Children

The attention you give to the following paragraphs depends upon the situation of you and your partner now, in relation to children in your marriage. Consider these possibilities and then explore those that apply to you: We plan never to have children; we plan to conceive or adopt children; we are expecting a child; or we now have children and may plan more. In each of these situations, there are special factors affecting the marriage relationship.

Choosing Not to Become Parents

Not every couple will choose to become parents. We hope every child will be a wanted child, although, unfortunately, some couples have parenthood thrust upon them. Couples may have good reasons for wanting to remain childless. Their careers may make parenthood difficult. Some partners may be involved in other helpful activities that are satisfying—perhaps working directly with other people's children. Some persons simply do not enjoy being with children or adolescents. Because some expect a married couple to have children, it may be difficult for you to explain your nonparent status. It is important that you both continue to be comfortable with your decision.

Plan to Have Children in the Future

If possible, living as a couple without others in the home for at least a year or two after your wedding allows you to adjust to each other before your children arrive.

There are many constructive reasons for wanting children. A woman and a man who are secure with each other as spouses may desire to share this love and happiness. Parenting involves a willingness to devote many years to caring for children and helping to grow into maturity.

Good parents treat their children as individuals with rights and dignity. As they seek to under-

---

EXPLORE 3.4A: Not Being Parents

If you and your partner do not want to become parents at any time in your marriage, discuss your reasons and feelings.

Talk with other couples who have made the same decision. What factors might cause you to change your mind later, perhaps when you are too old to have children?

When do you enjoy helping others' children? What past experiences, career motives, or other factors are involved in your decision? When, if ever, does either of you feel defensive about your nonparent status? How do you respond to those who expect you to have children?

EXPLORE 3.4B: Pregnancy

Talk with your partner about your feelings concerning pregnancy. Discuss the changes it brings.

How will, or do, you support each other during pregnancy? What will you do if you have an unexpected or unplanned pregnancy? Share your feelings and some of the sources of these feelings.

---

stand their growing children, they also discover new insights about themselves. Parenting may be for you if you enjoy children and like to play, work, and share with them.

Some couples may want children for poor reasons. A person who is lonely and hungry for love may want a child in order to receive affection. Some persons conceive children as a way to prove their sexual potency or to solve marriage problems. Children do not hold a marriage together. On the contrary, parenthood tests the commitment of spouses to each other and to the children. In many ways, the presence of children in your home places additional strain on your relationship as partners.

One objective of parents is to work themselves out of their parenting roles by enabling their children to become more independent and to enjoy life by themselves.

Now Pregnant

Although it is the woman who becomes pregnant, a pregnancy continues, as well as begins, as a couple matter.

You and your partner may have read and discussed the concerns mentioned in "Plan to Have Children in the Future."

EXPLORE 3.4C: Planning to Become Parents

With your partner, share your dreams and feelings about being parents. How will you balance your time and responsibilities for your children and spouse? These questions may be important to consider:

1. What are your reasons for wanting children?

2. What kinds of experiences with children have you had? Did you have younger brothers or sisters for whom you cared? How do you feel about your own family situations as they have involved children?

3. What do you hope, or fear, having children will be like? What do you want most to do with and/or for your children? How many daughters and/or sons do you want?

4. What if your child is severely limited or disabled in some way? Does either of you have a genetic history that indicates your children might inherit a disease or handicap? Have you carefully checked this possibility? Have you discussed it with appropriate medical experts? How do you feel about this?

5. If you do not already have children, are you able to conceive children? If you and your partner could not conceive, what alternatives would you consider? Would you adopt children? Would you consider artificial insemination?

If you never have conceived together, what if, perhaps after years of careful use of contraceptives, you discover that you cannot conceive? Discuss your feelings about these areas.

6. Suppose you have an unplanned pregnancy. How would this affect your other plans, such as changing jobs, moving, or completing additional education? Under what circumstances would you seek an abortion, if at all? What backup plans and resources do you have for this possibility?

Pregnancy is not a disease, and it can be an exciting time with partners coming to appreciate each other in new ways. In addition, together with other expectant couples, spouses can participate in prenatal and childbirth classes. It is essential to secure adequate prenatal care as early as possible.

Although pregnancy is not an adequate reason for marriage, some couples may feel pressured to marry because they are already pregnant. With a premarital pregnancy, it is essential for the couple to think about other alternatives, as well as marriage, with a minister or counselor.

Now Have Children and May Have More

If you and/or your partner have children from a previous marriage, many additional factors are involved in your own marriage. For some couples, there are decisions about child support and visitation rights by the ex-spouse. Deciding with which parent the children will live is essential yet often difficult. There are also decisions about the new partner's adoption of his or her mate's children and about involvement in parenting. The parent's new spouse becomes, in many ways, an "instant parent."

If you have children from a previous marriage and you plan to have more children with your current partner, the ages of the children sometimes may become a factor. Much depends upon how each partner feels about the present children, as compared to future children. When partners work together in helping children adjust to the new marriage, blended families can be just as successful as others. If parents tend to consider each child as "his" or "hers," then these underlying attitudes of fear and uncertainty may make adjustments more difficult.

EXPLORE 3.4D: Instant Parents and Blended Families

If you and/or your partner now have children, you probably have discussed and experienced the way they affect your relationship. How do you balance your time and responsibilities for your children and spouse? Consider these issues:

1. Describe your feelings about each child. What effects has each made in your relationship? Do the ages and genders of your children make a difference?

2. If you are divorced and have children from your previous marriage, what revisions in child support, visitation rights, and other areas will you make in relation to your current marriage? Discuss the feelings between your new partner and former spouse(s).

3. If you are widowed, talk about the way your adjustments relate to your partner now. What reactions do your children have to your new marriage?

4. How do your children feel about having a "new" mother or father? In your current relationship, how will you, your partner, and your children relate to "ex-relatives" who are still related through the children?

5. What legal, financial, or property matters do you need to consider, in relation to your children and your new marriage? If you have a will, are revisions needed in it? If you do not have a will, now is the time to prepare it, regardless of your age.

6. If you plan to have children with your new partner, either by birth or by adoption, what reactions might your present children have?

7. If both partners have children from previous marriages, which residence will you use: his, hers, or a new "neutral" place? What issues are involved in helping the different sets of children blend into one family?

8. How will you share your faith and spiritual perspectives with your children? In what ways will you encourage them to participate in church activities?

When I was a child, I spoke like a child, I thought like a child, I reasoned like a child; when I became an adult, I put an end to childish ways. *(1 Corinthians 13:11, NRSV)*

Marriage and parenthood are living parables that enable us to better understand God's grace and love.

Your Family as a Caring Community

This is a positive opportunity for you and your partner to consider your children, and any others in your household, as members of a cooperative team of persons who share mutual support, love, and care for one another, and work together for the good of all. This cooperation is not automatic; it takes attitudes of love and respect to develop this caring community in which a gain for one is a gain for all, and a sadness or loss for one affects all who are involved.

This covenant perspective offers you support as you consider whether to have children and/or how best to parent the children you already have. You provide important models for your children, yet you encourage them to absorb the good characteristics of others, as well. You affirm your children and other relatives, yet you know there are others who also care. It is a relief to realize that, as a parent, you do not have to do everything alone. You are not the only emotional support for your children.

The fellowship of the church helps you in your marriage and as parents. The Christian community, at its best, expresses this graceful relationship between persons, regardless of age, sex, status, or other characteristics. Within the context of the church as the household of God, your marriage and family can be the church in your home.

Your Marriage Is First

A key to successful parenthood is that you, the spouses, keep your marriage relationship fresh and alive as the basic bond of the family. When your marriage relationship is healthy, you are able to place the additional demands of parenting in better focus. This builds trust and openness. With respect between both parents, children can love and respect each parent as individuals and are not forced to choose between parents.

Regular periods alone together will help you maintain a growing and enjoyable relationship. Finding couple privacy may be difficult, but essential. Many couples schedule at least one night out each week as a couple. These parents arrange for child care so that these occasions can be pleasant. Many churches have couples' groups that schedule social activities and provide nurseries and separate activities for the children.

Take time to encourage your love and romance as a couple. This provides a stronger basis for the love you then can share with your children. As the children mature and leave home, these couple times become even more significant for you.

Basic Parenting Skills

Marriage and parenting are interrelated in many ways. Here we invite you to talk about a few basic principles. Additional resources are listed in the back of this book. You can explore more details through parent education programs in your community. Your church, support couples, minister, school, and other organizations may provide parent education opportunities or give you information about them.

Good parenting does not just happen or come naturally. For better or worse, we learn parenting skills from our childhood family experiences, from talking with others and observing how they relate to their children. Our children will learn many of their parenting skills from us, and we will see their effects on our grandchildren!

You will use many of the same skills and qualities in parenting you develop in your husband-wife relationship. Patience, forgiveness, empathy, and communication are just as important between parents and children as they are between husband and wife. Expectations, attitudes, and feelings are still the basic elements that guide your behaviors as a parent. Knowing what to expect from your children in their normal development at each age gives a healthy perspective to parenting so you can be more confident in difficult times. Your family experiences can become times of growth for all concerned, rather than episodes of despair and destructiveness.

Parenting Constantly Changes

The ways in which we parent are constantly changing according to the ages and experiences of each child. What works for one child may not work as well for another. Parents must make many decisions on behalf of their young children. Even in preschool years children already assume some of these decisions, such as what they want to eat or wear and how they will interact with others. As children experience the consequences of their actions, they develop a sense of structure and personal responsibility and limits.

When children enter school, they assume many more responsibilities and choices with less direct supervision from their parents. By teenage years, parents transfer most decision-making to their emerging adolescents. Letting go of children frees them to come back to you. By high school graduation, the adolescent is ready to assume full adulthood responsibilities, including where to live, how to earn money, what to study, how to use time, which friends to choose, and most of the tasks of adulthood.

Parenting shifts from parent-child to adult-adult, from being in total control of a child's life in preschool years to being a respected friend and consultant in high school years and beyond. As you have become adults and moved from your parents' homes to enter marriage and form your own home, so we hope your children can some day do the same when they become adults.

The difficulty of parenting often is in knowing when to hold on to a given standard and when to allow children to make their own decisions and experience the results—how to balance structure and freedom. Experiencing these dilemmas as parents can help us to appreciate God's dilemmas in giving us freedom to grow yet keeping us from being so hurt or damaged that we give up on life.

Three Parenting Guidelines

Three brief principles are keys to parenting.

1. Now Is Most Important

The most important time of your child's life is right now, because it is the only time available for you to be with your children. In order to influence the future, now is the time to share your knowledge and love. The standards your children observe in you will continue with them to others, forming a rich return on the care and love you have invested.

2. Modeling Is Teaching

Describe the type of person you want your child to be, and then be like that person. In this way, your example demonstrates behavior your child can copy. What you are speaks so loudly that your children cannot hear what you say. Your children learn most from seeing the way you live every day. Being a model does not mean you must be perfect. It means you share yourself with your children. You share the good, and you also show the way you respond when things go wrong and you are less than you would like to be.

Every child needs a sense of love and security, experiences of success, and a good self-image. Dependable care helps your children to feel confident and succeed in most of their life's endeavors, whether large or small. Through your example, you enable a child to form a good self-image as a member of a family and teach them to be competent and capable, so they can grow comfortably into adulthood.

EXPLORE 3.4E: Parenting

Talk about how you are applying (or will apply) these three parenting principles:
> Now is important.
> Modeling is teaching.
> Children are persons.

What have you learned from your own parents and relatives about parenting skills? Which of these do you want to use with your children? Which do you want to modify or omit?

A simple rule for parenting:
> Describe the type of adult you want your child to be, and then be that adult yourself.
> How are you applying this principle in your own parenting and other child care?

3. *Children Are Persons*

Relatives, In-Laws, Friends

Children need a balance of structure and freedom. They have a right to privacy and to physical safety. As you involve your children in decisions that affect them and the family, you help them assume responsibility as worthwhile individuals.

Parents do not own their children. Parents are only the nurturing and care-giving custodians for their children on behalf of God. We care for our children as stewards of God, the great parent of us all. We see God in the image of our parents, just as our image of God guides us in being parents to our children. When children experience their parents as good, such as being dependable, fair, forgiving, consistent, caring, trustworthy, and understanding, they have a foundation for relating to God as good and loving. If children experience their parents as bad, such as being hurtful, angry, rejecting, and cold, they are more likely to see God as vengeful, distant, or uncaring.

When sharp triangles exist, it is difficult to maintain a happy family circle. Triangles sometimes occur between you, your partner, and your children. As adult children of your parents, you, your partner, and either set of in-laws may have three-sided conflicts. As you discovered in Theme One, you each bring your experiences with family members and others into your marriage. Parents, brothers, sisters, and other relatives, although they may be absent or deceased, still influence you through the attitudes and habits you learned from them. These continuing inner voices sometimes are called your "parent tapes." Therefore, it is important that you and your partner continue to talk openly with each other about all your family relationships.

Frequent contact between you, your partner, and relatives provides greater opportunity to be caught between their requests and your own desires. Living near relatives, working at the same place, or having

EXPLORE 3.4F: Relations With Relatives

With your partner, discuss issues that are important for you in your interaction with your relatives. Some of these questions may help you explore those areas:

1. Where would you most like to live, in relation to the residences of your parents or other relatives?

2. Where and how will, or do, you celebrate holidays, birthdays, and other special occasions? Which would you like to vary in some way?

3. How do you feel about your relatives? Your blood relations are your partner's in-laws. What difference, if any, does this make in the way you each relate to your partner's relatives? Earlier you may have explored the good and not so good characteristics of several important relatives. Talk more about these family members and the way you feel about them.

4. What special problems will, or do, you have with certain relatives? Some of these might be: earning more or less than they do, being in a different career or type of work, involvement in a family business or other joint activity, chronic health conditions, care for older relatives, family financial obligations, emergencies, differences in life view and philosophy.

5. In what ways are you good friends with your relatives and in-laws? What are important conflicts you have with them?

6. How have marriages, divorces, deaths, and other events affected the way you feel about family members? If you have a blended family, with several sets of grandparents and other relatives, how would you like to relate to each set of relatives? Which among these relatives do your children prefer?

7. How do you each react to what your parents and other relatives say about your partner or you? In relation to your relatives, what does it mean for you to "forsake all others" for your spouse?

them live in your home brings complications for you and your partner to resolve together. You and your partner also probably have some unfinished deep emotional involvements with your parents or other relatives. The arrival of your own children or the aging of your parents may sensitize you to these underlying feelings.

Most adults move through three stages of relationship with their parents—from dependence in childhood, to independence as adolescents, and finally to interdependence and cooperation, as between equals, in adulthood. Often a person is in some part of each of these three stages, depending upon the issue at hand. Sometimes conflicts between partners result because one partner continues to have excessive emotional dependency on his or her own parents or other relatives. You need to be free from your parents in the sense of not being dependent as their children, so you can be closer to them as the adults you are now. Shifting your relationship from parent/child to adult/adult may be difficult, especially if your parents have their own unresolved emotional investments in you as their children. Assuming adult roles with parents can be more complicated if they have health or housing needs that their adult children are expected to resolve.

Extended Family Possibilities

A man leaves his father and his mother and clings to his wife, and they become one flesh.
(Genesis 2:24, NRSV)

Therefore what God has joined together, let no one separate. *(Mark 10:9, NRSV)*

These biblical statements affirm the covenant of marriage as the central relationship that defines extended families and the relationships between family generations. On the basis of blood and legal ties, an extended family includes single adults, married couples, and children. When you and your partner clearly define your family relationships, you can then appreciate your extended families for the many important positive supports that family members can share with one another.

The church community is similar to the larger extended family. An extended family includes all sizes and types of homes and families. The church's emphasis upon love, forgiveness, and concern for all helps to create a supportive network of caring persons who are available to children and to their parents. You may have had negative experiences with some churches that failed to reach these ideals, yet place these negatives in the larger context of God's call to express love, care, and forgiveness.

When relatives are few or live far away, couples who want family support and experiences can obtain these through a church group, or they can organize a family cluster. A family cluster usually includes several couples and their children, as well as single and divorced persons of various ages. Children whose own grandparents are not easily available can benefit from having substitute grandparents in the family cluster or from other activities in a church. This offers ways for couples and their children to participate in a mutual support system with others. Letters and long distance calls to parents or other relatives can also give support during difficult times as well as sharing happiness in times of joy.

Friends

Not all your friends will be, nor need be, mutual friends. Some are closer than family. Since you and your partner are individuals and have your own interests, it is enriching for each of you to have some separate friendships. These may develop around hobbies, recreational activities, social clubs, or job-related interests. Sharing your experiences from these friendships can expand the quality of your marriage.

Sometimes a lack of friendships may suggest you are uncomfortable with other persons. If you do not have other friends, too heavy a burden may be placed upon your partner to provide all the emotional support you need. Mutual interests or physical location help form common bonds and support the virtues you hold. Your pattern of friendships will change due to interests, moves, job changes, and other factors.

EXPLORE 3.4G: Friends

With your partner, take some time to consider the way your friendships relate to your marriage. Use these questions to guide you:

1. Select two or three friends who have meant much to you. Describe the qualities you value in each friend. You might tell your partner about the most enjoyable or the funniest experience you had with each friend.

2. Which of your friends does your partner especially like or dislike? Do you dislike any of your partner's friends? Describe the feelings you each have about these friends.

3. Are there times when you prefer to be with your friend(s) rather than with your partner? In what ways do these times help or threaten your relationship?

4. Do you or your partner discuss "private" matters with any friends? Is this acceptable to you? . . . to your partner?

5. Do you and your partner quarrel or disagree in the presence of friends? When? Does either of you try to out talk, control, embarrass the other, or do you act differently when your friends are present? How do each of you feel about these times?

6. Which activities do you enjoy doing with friends—individually and/or as a couple?

7. What are your agreements, or ground rules, concerning possible sexual facets of friendships? Does either of you worry about a possible sexual or romantic involvement of your partner with others? How might loneliness, feelings of rejection, or other emotional factors affect your friendships? Talk about your feelings and reactions in these areas.

8. What expressions of warmth, appreciation, and affection are appropriate between you and your friends? . . . between your partner and his or her friends ?

9. Does time you each spend with friends interfere with your relationship as partners? If so, describe when this happens and how you would like to change it.

10. Do your friendships include persons from several racial and ethnic groups? How do your friendships express your standards and goals? In what way are your friendships related to your community, church, or career involvements?

Searching the Possibilities

Relatives may bring potential problems, yet they also offer unlimited possibilities for growth in love and concern. Your marriage is a part of your individual family systems. Although relations with relatives often appear to be triangles, with two against one, they provide an opportunity for you and your partner to blend and expand your lives into circles of love and care, with your children and with others. In this way you create your own joint family system.

The continuing search for answers to the dilemmas of security versus freedom, concern for self versus concern for others, and the keeping of traditions versus the creation of new traditions, is part of normal family relationships.

3.5

WORK, CAREER, VOCATION

Go into all the world. God calls each of us to service in the world. Whether paid or volunteer, your work can be your response to God's call to you to minister and care for others.

Some Dimensions of Work

There are at least six dimensions involved in choosing or in changing your work and career.

Interests include what you enjoy doing and what you dislike.

Abilities are what you can do well; your work skills.

Goals are your objectives in life: What you would like to have achieved five years from now or twenty years from now.

Expectations involve what job or career others want you to pursue.

Opportunities involve whether some business or other unit of society will pay you to do what you want to do and can do.

Rewards are results from combining these elements.

Career Development Stages

You will have new opportunities for creative choices and satisfying work, which you may be unable to see at the present time.

Across your lifetime, your jobs will change, the meanings you attach to your work will change, and the needs of society for certain types of work will also change.

The stages summarized here assume that individuals have opportunities, access to necessary training, and receive encouragement to develop appropriate work skills. Career-stages also are affected by the increasing opportunities for people to set their own time agendas for paid work, family, and other involvements.

Pre-career preparation is the stage when trade school, college, professional, or other training is obtained, to prepare for entry-level positions in specific occupational areas.

EXPLORE 3.5A: Meanings of Work

Take time with your partner to exchange feelings and attitudes toward yourselves and work. These guides may help:

1. How does your job, occupation, or career express the person you are? Does it mean more to you than just a way to earn money?

2. Together, consider Jesus' story of the three persons who had different talents (money or abilities) in Matthew 25:14-30. Talk also about the meaning of the statement, "Where your treasure is, there will your heart be also" (Matthew 6:21).

3. What do you do, paid or not paid, that gives you a sense of being valuable and worthwhile?

4. Share the way you feel when you cannot do the work you want to do. What if you cannot find satisfying work or cannot find any job at all? How do you deal with disappointments and dissatisfaction in your work?

Entry level is the first few years in which a person gains experience. These job positions require minimum preparation and no experience. Job transfers within a company, or from one company to another, maybe from one beginning position to another.

Establishment and advancement is a period during which a person achieves promotions, gains more status and authority in a line of work, and moves to a maximum level of competence and security.

Maintenance or reassessment is on the basis of earlier achievements. In this period a person continues at a high level of work productivity, which often includes management responsibility or owning their own business.

Retirement or re-engagement includes the realistic assessment of one's individual work abilities, interests, and opportunities for continued work. While official retirement concludes work careers for many, continued employment or alternate occupations are options for others.

Your Three Vocations

The root word for *vocation* is "to call" or "to make vocal." Your vocation is one way to make your personality known in the world about you. It is your calling.

You have at least three vocations, or callings, from God. What is the relative importance of each for you now?

1. As a person, your challenge *to become the best person you can be* is basic to marriage, family, work, church, leisure, and other areas of life.

2. *Your marriage* is to create and to bring to reality some of the many potentials that are possible with your partner.

3. *Your work or career*, through which you contribute to the world beyond self and family, is for pay or as a volunteer.

Which Comes First?

Job requirements, especially, may raise power and priority issues for you and your partner. Advancement in your career field may require overtime and intensive work away from home. Your employer may expect you to give your job priority over your marriage, but you and your partner may want to place your relationship first. You may be forced to choose between marriage and job priorities at times when it is difficult to make those decisions. It is essential to continue to talk with each other about these issues.

EXPLORE 3.5B: Career-Planning Issues

Take some relaxed time to talk with your partner about issues that are important to you and your relationship. You may want to make some notes independently and then come together to talk about them.

1. What is your current career? What are your plans? What do you imagine you will be doing in ten years? Are you now at a midlife or second-career transition?

2. How would you like your spouse to feel about your work, both paid and volunteer? What problems and possibilities will the work of each partner present for your marriage?

3. Consider the way job factors, such as hours, work schedules, travel, necessary clothes, work associates, opportunities, pay, location, and required moves to new communities, may affect your marriage. Is the job dangerous or tension-producing? Is it worthwhile to you? to your partner? to others?

4. Do you have the education necessary for your careers? How does each partner feel about additional training that may be required or desirable? What crises might unexpectedly alter your career plans? Discuss these and the way you can prepare for them.

5. How important is the income from your job in comparison to the type work it is, your enjoyment of it, and its prestige? With your income, can you finance your marriage in the way you would like?

6. Will (or does) your job involve working with a parent, relative, or close friend? If so, what possible conflicts might develop between you, your partner, and these other persons?

Change Stresses the System

Competing demands of work often stress marriage. You can reduce stress by acknowledging these sources of fatigue and deciding which ones you will accept as being who you are and which cycles you can modify. Modifying any part of a system may produce unexpected changes in the individual or in the couple.

Conflicts, crises, disagreements, and problems increase your levels of stress and fatigue.

A couple or a family system works very much like an individual system. As an individual, your bodily systems have adapted to a typical, or normal, level of stimulation and stress. Too little stress allows the system to degenerate or "rust out." Too little excitement tends to produce boredom, listlessness, and feelings of rejection.

Too much stress produces anxiety, worry, frustration, and fatigue. Both extremes may lead to a loss of confidence and dissatisfaction.

Burnout and Depression

Constant fatigue and burnout may be early signs of depression, a combination of biological and situational factors. Depression may be a reaction to disappointments in work or family when things don't go the way you want or hoped. When depression does not clear up with rest and a slower pace, then a more serious chronic depression may be present. When fatigue and stress seems beyond your control it is time to consult a physician or therapist who understands the interpersonal, psychological, and physical aspects of human behavior.

Three Stages of Stress

Alarm and Awareness

There are three basic stages in reaction to increased stress. In the first stage, stress on an individual (or a couple) produces an initial alarm reaction. Shifts in feelings and behaviors call attention to the problem and may result in increased alertness, greater sensitivity, muscle tension, and other reactions that are needed to cope with what may be a possible threat to the system.

Resistance and Coping

Here the individual (or the couple) draws on skills and resources to correct the situation. If this action is successful, the system returns to its normal level of operation. Energy then can be renewed through relaxation and rest, and the full strength of the individual (or couple) is ready for other activities or the next stress.

Exhaustion and Defeat

If the coping behaviors of stage two are not sufficient to overcome the stress, fatigue increases, a sense of frustration, anxiety, and inadequacy develops, which may produce additional secondary stress. If a new stress occurs while the person (or couple) is in this stage, it will add greatly to the feeling of being overwhelmed. Sometimes fatigue produces illness, and this may have the side benefit of removing the person from the initial stressful situation.

EXPLORE 3.5C: Stress Responses

Allow some time for you and your partner to review some of the recent changes you have had in your lives. Talk about how stressful each change was, or is, and the way you each responded to it. What specific actions did you take to cope with the stress?

Discuss a major positive change, such as changing your residence, your wedding, or birth of a child. What factors might present problems for you?

Consider the possible changes you may face in the next few weeks or months. Which changes, such as a different job or moving, might be most stressful? How will you cope with those stresses? Which pleasant, desirable changes also might be stressful for you?

Work, Marriage, and Family Issues

The challenges of relating your work/career and your marriage/family involve all four themes of faith, hope, love, and power. Your personal identity as a spouse and family member, and your career identity as a worker, whether as a laborer, manager, professional, owner, or investor, call you to make decisions that express your values and priorities—your faith.

Your vision for your future guides your goals, accomplishments, failures, choices, and plans in both your career and your marriage and family. As you seek to love and care for others, you face many choices about doing what is best for yourself, your spouse and family, and for others at work, in your community, and the world about you. Your power

to make good things happen depends not only upon your communication and conflict resolution skills but also on having the necessary skills and qualifications to do the work for which you are paid as well as the volunteer unpaid services that you give.

God has created us as free persons with a finite presence in this world, limited by time and space, often most obvious in the requirements of marriage and of career. As you consider how to manage your career/occupation/ work/job requirements in relation to your marriage and family covenant, this is your opportunity to get a larger overview of the many ways that faith, hope, love, and power guide your career, marriage, and personal development.

EXPLORE 3.5D: Person, Marriage, and Career Priorities

Your work, marriage, and personal identity interface in many ways. These are magnified when both spouses have paid and/or volunteer work obligations. Talk together about issues that produce conflict or stress for you and/or your spouse. Describe the solutions you can use to reduce conflicts and increase your marriage and career satisfaction.

1. How do the values of your work associates and managers fit with your marriage and family values? Which friendships threaten or support your marriage? How do conflicts at work impact your marriage?

2. How flexible are your work schedules? Does your work require hours of commuting, extended travel away from home, overtime, or emergency duties? When work requires most of your time in some weeks, can you schedule extra time to be with each other to make up for missed family time?

3. If you have children, how do (or will) you manage childcare and work obligations? How will each parent be available to children each day and week? How will you handle health or emergencies?

4. How do you use the internet, e-mail, cell phones, and other technologies to do work at home or other non-work locations? How do you keep these technologies from usurping time for your marriage, family, and leisure?

5. When your career involves changing companies, additional job training, or moving to a different location, how do (or will) you cope with these changes? If one spouse must move to obtain a promotion or salary increase but the change of residence would damage the career of the other spouse, how will you resolve these conflicts?

6. Discuss other career and marriage issues that you now face or may face in the future.

Theme Four

POWER THROUGH COMMUNICATION

Let us love one another,
for those who love their spouses as neighbors fulfill the law.
(paraphrase from Romans 12:8-12)

The fruit of the Spirit is love, joy, peace, patience, kindness,
generosity, faithfulness, gentleness, and self-control.
(Galatians 5:22-23, NRSV)

Grant that I may not so much seek to be consoled, as to console;
to be understood, as to understand;
to be loved, as to love . . .
from the Prayer of Saint Francis of Assisi

The covenant of marriage was established by God, who created us male and female for each
other. With his presence and power Jesus graced a wedding at Cana of Galilee, and in his
sacrificial love gave us the example for the love of husband and wife.
(From the "Service of Christian Marriage," The United Methodist Hymnal, *pages 864–69)*

EXPLORE 4: Some Definitions of Power

You may read some references from the Bible, such as 1 Corinthians 7, Ephesians 5, Galatians 3, and talk about how they relate to your marriage. Talk about some of these concepts and find other Scriptures, stories, proverbs, and other descriptions of marriage.

The word *power* has many definitions and variations. In the following list, independently circle the words and phrases that best define power for you. Then talk together regarding your choices.

strength	control	possibilities	sensitive	competent
resources	energy	schedule	options	aggression
skills	abilities	learning	money	knowledge
personality	appearance	sex	authority	manipulation
destruction	building up	force	support	improvements

4.1
POWER, LISTENING, EXPRESSING

Healthy Expression of Power

You each express power in different ways. In some couples, the partner who talks more, or louder, or sulks, or says nothing, or complains tends to control the outcome of events in the marriage. With other couples, one partner may use money, sex, criticism, or hurtful remarks to control the relationship.

By contrast, strength can be freeing and uplifting when partners seek a result or goal that is enjoyable for both. Being pleasant expresses a positive confidence and support of self and partner. The old saying that "honey catches more flies than vinegar" suggests that partners can choose to use their power in constructive, beneficial ways for each other and for others.

In your marriage it is not a matter of whether you have or do not have power. It is a matter of using it in constructive, rather than destructive, ways. Each of you has the power to speak for yourself. No one takes power away from you. As you work out who makes which decisions in your relationship, you may mutually agree that one spouse usually will make certain types of decisions.

Control and Sensitivity

Control includes being sensitive to the wishes and rights of your partner and of others. When you know which outcomes you want—which are your goals—and if you are able to cause those desired outcomes to become a reality, then you probably will feel satisfied and happy in your marriage. You and your partner will measure your satisfaction with your marriage by comparing what you expect with what actually happens.

Communication through words and actions is your power to express love. Your resources, such as personality, knowledge, money, appearance, habits, and skills, give you potential (available) power. Power involves ability, strength, control, and energy.

The basic issue in power is finding balances between autonomy and cooperation, between being individuals and being a married couple, between

---

EXPLORE 4.1A: Sharing Your Power

Allow sufficient time to talk about the way you use your power and make decisions concerning your lives. It is important that you both decide together how you will use your skills and strengths in your marriage.

First, list several areas in which you are required to make decisions. These may concern essentials, such as budget, money, career, having and raising children, and sexual activities. Other areas may be hobbies, vacations, and use of leisure time. Each partner may make a separate list and then the lists may be compared.

Next, talk about the assumption you each hold about which of you makes the major decisions in those areas. How much input does each partner have on these decisions?

Although others may not actually be present in your lives now, they may continue to control your relationship. How much influence do others have over your marriage?

I know you believe you understand what you think I said,
But I am not sure you realize that what you heard is not what I meant.

Tell me you love me; it's so nice to hear. . . .

concern for your own needs and concern for the needs of your spouse. Controlled power is your ability and skill to cause things to happen as you want, both together and individually.

Communication: Words and Actions

You communicate by what you do and by what you say. Facial expressions and body posture and position express many meanings. The tone and pitch of your voice, your silences and gestures, often speak more loudly than words, although words are very important.

Inaccurate messages or conflicting messages often occur because you are using more than one channel to send information to your partner. Words may express positive affection, but the tone of voice and facial expression may be sending negative feelings. The same word may have different meanings for each partner at different times.

Sending and Receiving Messages

Verbal communication consists of what you say and how you say it. Content and process are important. Being a skilled listener is just as necessary as speaking effectively. You and your partner have accurate communication when you achieve a common meaning, based on messages that you send and receive.

It is very difficult, but not impossible, to alter your ways of communicating. You have developed your communication patterns over many years. To change some of these habits requires time and much practice. The brief information that follows can help you examine the way you and your partner communicate now. More complete aids for improving your couple-communication skills are available from many sources. Consult with your minister, support couples, and websites about workshops and other aids.

EXPLORE 4.1B: Beyond Words

To examine your channels of communication further, consider each method listed below. In each category, specify a behavior and describe its meaning for you.

Spoken Words: exclamations, tone of voice, volume, pet phrases, words you use often to describe many different things

Written Words: notes you send to each other, greeting cards, special ways of writing, symbols you use, designs

Facial Expressions: smiles, frowns, movement of lips or eyebrows, angle of head, or chin

Body Positions: posture, ways you sit or walk, position of your arms, hands, or legs

Touches: handclasps, backrubs, tender touches, texture of hands, hugs, other types of touches

Space: distance you sit or stand from each other, arrangement of furniture in your rooms

Time: schedules, being rushed or late for appointments, importance of time to each person

Other Channels: things you see, sounds, tastes, smells, ways you dress, grooming, and use of cosmetics

Begin with the channels that are easier to explore. Continue into other channels that are more difficult or threatening. Talk together about how it feels to focus on this aspect of communication and about what you learned about each other.

Three Steps to Effective Communication

When the impact on the listener matches the speaker's intent, you have accurate communication. In communicating as a sender (or speaker), your aim is to enable another person to understand your intended message. As a receiver (or listener), your aim is to understand the speaker's meaning accurately. When you focus first on your process you can then get to content and solutions. Effective communication results in mutual understanding. Your communication is effective when your message is described accurately by your partner, and you both have the same understanding of its meaning.

Whether your message is positive or negative, the important skill is your ability to express it so your partner, as the listener, can understand it. Your partner then can respond by becoming the sender, while you listen. Your partner's response to your message is, itself, a new message.

There are three observable steps in communicating a message. First, the speaker sends a clear message to the listener. Next, the listener interprets or restates the sender's message by summarizing its main points. Last, the sender confirms that the listener's summary is accurate.

If the listener's summary is incomplete, the speaker restates the message as needed until both sender and receiver are sure they agree on the message. This is confirming the feedback. It is the sender's responsibility to convey a clear message that is brief enough that the listener can summarize it easily. It is the listener's responsibility to attempt to summarize the sender's whole message, without adding anything to it until both sender and receiver agree on the intended meaning.

These three steps result in a shared common meaning or mutual understanding. The sender knows that the listener has received the message accurately, and the listener knows that the sender has confirmed the accuracy of the listener's interpretation.

In most conversations these three steps are so rapid that the important feedback and confirmation steps may not be noticed. When they are missing, however, communication breaks down, or more correctly, messages are misunderstood or missed completely.

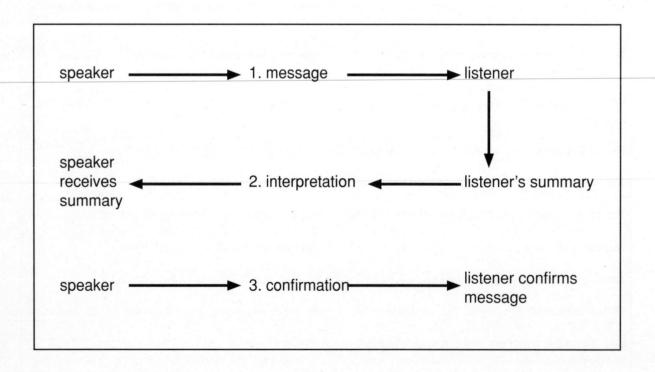

"I" and "You" Messages

"You" is a tricky pronoun that can be used to confuse or accuse. When used to identify the listener in relation to the speaker, "you" is a very helpful pronoun. Partners sometimes confuse or misuse "you" when they really mean "I." A person may say, "When you go to the store and you see the high prices, you worry about having enough money to live." The speaker here is probably referring to self, not the listener. A more accurate statement would be, "When I go to the store and I see the high prices, I worry about having enough money to live." This second statement gives a clear "I message" about the speaker's inner feelings and perceptions.

A second misuse of "you" occurs when individuals say "you" in an accusing, demanding way. Some examples are, "You should believe this," or "You're dumb," or "You ought to love me more," or "You can't be serious." These types of "you messages" imply that the speaker is demanding, dominating, or manipulating the listener in some way. As a result the listener may feel that the speaker does not value her or him.

Partners can replace "you messages" with non-blaming statements, such as, "I wish you would believe this" or "I'm surprised."

Often phrases that include or imply "you should," "you ought," or "you must" carry underlying messages from the speaker, blaming or accusing the listener. (For more details on these concepts, consult references in the back of the book.)

When you send a message, it contains your understandings, feelings, desires, and plans that you are expressing to your listener. When you are the receiver of a message, you add your own reactions to the messages you hear.

It helps when you use "I" to refer to your own inner self-awareness and "you" to refer to your partner's behaviors and statements. This may seem very simple—perhaps unnecessary—but using "I" and "you" in these better ways can improve your communication.

Send More Accurate Messages

Both sender and receiver can help to make a message clearer and more accurate. As a sender, be sure to include these elements in your message (the exact order is not important).

Sense Data: In specific terms, describe the situation or event to which you refer, reporting what you saw, heard, touched, smelled, or tasted.

Meanings: Describe the interpretation (or meaning) that you give to the event.

Feelings: Describe how you felt at the time, and how you feel now about the event. Be alert to your hidden feelings.

Intentions: Describe what you intend or what you want to do (or not to do) as your response to the event or situation.

Actions: State clearly what you have decided, and the request (if any) you are making of your partner. (Don't assume that your partner knows what you want.) Here is an example:

> "When you *said* you were sorry but you *did not* reach out and hug me" (the specific event or message), "I *felt* confused and left out because I *thought* you did not realize how important this is for me" (sender's feelings and interpretations of the event). So "I *wanted* to back off from you" (sender's intention connected to perception of the event).

Notice that "you" is used only to refer to what the other person actually did, not to what the other person thought, felt, or wanted.

The above statement is an example of an accurate "I message," explaining the way the speaker's understanding of the situation was formed. It allows the listener to report his or her own views of the same event, without needing to defend against accusations from the speaker.

The focus is on an observable event and the sender's responses to it. Of course, when the listener becomes the sender, she or he will focus on the same event and share her or his feelings, interpretations, and intentions.

Note that the better phrase is not "You did not realize" but, "I *thought you* did not realize" to report one's interpretation (decoding) of an event. The speaker is not assuming anything that might be going on inside the other person, which the speaker cannot know.

Good Listening Helps

Rephrasing: As a receiver, you can help your partner send more accurate messages by rephrasing the words so that she or he can confirm the accuracy of your understanding. This helps the sender know that you understand how the sender sees the situation.

As listener, you can use the same five elements mentioned before as the basis for questions to the sender, when part of the message seems to be missing. You may invite your sending partner to be clearer by asking: "Which events are you describing?" "Did you really want that to happen?" "How did you feel about what happened?"

Respect: Your covenant in marriage includes mutual respect. In looking closely at a difficult situation, each of you needs the opportunity to express views openly and without criticism. If you feel mutually accepted as a team, it is easier to make the effort to achieve an accurate understanding of a situation and to gain a shared meaning.

Trouble Shooting

When a relationship becomes troubled, it is usually because the partners are communicating negative messages of rejection—not because they are not communicating at all. At other times, difficulties occur because partners cannot "hear" each other because of fears and hurts from previous experiences.

In your discussions, seek to hear and understand each other, but do not try to dominate or convince. You can hear the other's viewpoint without judging whether it is right or wrong. Be careful not to manipulate, coerce, or force your partner, but listen carefully and try to describe to your partner what you hear him or her saying.

EXPLORE 4.1C: Changing the Meanings of Words

Take a few minutes with your partner and select a word or a brief phrase, such as, "This is really important to me." Then repeat this phrase to your partner several times, using various vocal emphases, voice pitches, speeds, or volumes to convey each of the different meanings suggested here:

Meaning 1. You really appreciate your partner.
Meaning 2. You actually are displeased with your partner.
Meaning 3. You affirm your partner, whether others do or not.
Meaning 4. You are unsure about yourself or about your partner.
Meaning 5. You want your partner to do something for you.

After you both have tried this exercise, talk about the changes you made in order to convey each meaning.

EXPLORE 4.1D: Beyond Words

Sometimes it is difficult to get from negatives to positives. Here is a way to succeed as you clarify your feelings and wants. You may call this your "Here and Now Wheel."

First draw a circle, then write two words that describe the good or pleasant feelings you have right now. Then write two words or phrases that describe negative or unpleasant feelings you now have. These can be placed in the four parts of your wheel, like this:

Pleasant Feelings

Unpleasant Feelings

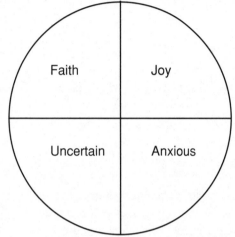

Next, write a sentence using all four feeling words, connecting them in a meaningful way. Together you can talk about the statement you have made. In the above example, one possible sentence could be: "When I am uncertain, my faith helps me to feel joy, so I am less anxious."

Each partner can try several sets of words and phrases about feelings. You might also share your sentences with others in a couples' group.

Use this procedure to become aware of your feelings, standards, goals, and desires. Note how positives often outweigh negatives. (*This exercise was suggested by Gwen White, a member of the editorial committee for the 1981 edition of this book.*)

There Is More to Communicating

In this chapter we have suggested some important factors of good communication between you and your partner. There are many more, yet books are inadequate to assist you in changing your basic communication habits. We encourage you to participate in couple-growth opportunities that are available through churches and other community sources. Your minister or counselor can suggest couple enrichment opportunities, and you also may request information from the sources listed in the back of this book.

Your ways of communicating express the covenant you make as partners in marriage. Techniques are important, yet your attitudes and love for each other determine the way you will use your skills for communicating.

Good communication skills are essential for your growth. Problem solving is one of the major ways in which you grow as individuals and as a couple.

4.2

FEEDBACK FOR CHANGE

Intent, Impact, and Feedback

Intent includes the information you want your partner to know, the emotions you want to elicit from your partner, and a request for your partner to act in some way.

Impact is what your partner experiences, feels, and does in response to the messages you communicate. You can only control your intent and the ways you encode your intent into messages to your partner. You cannot control how your partner decodes your messages and then chooses to respond to you.

Accurate communication occurs when the *impact* of your message on your partner *matches* your original *intent*. Accurate communication is neither good nor bad. What makes a message good or bad is the intention of the message sender in combination with the effects on the listener who receives the message.

External communication problems may have their source in your choice of particular words that have different meanings for your partner than they do for you.

Internal sources of communication difficulties have more to do with your attitude toward your part-

ner. You may assume your partner does not value and love you; as a result, you may misinterpret some messages. At other times, you may assume you are correct but your partner is wrong, so you may not try to find a common meaning in the message.

Match Words and Meanings

Meanings are in persons, not in words. When you have thoughts, feelings, desires, and other meanings that you wish to share with your partner, put them into a form your partner can understand. To do this, package your message into words, gestures, and facial expressions that form the message your partner can see, hear, and touch. This is encoding your message. Your words and body language carry your message.

As the listener, your partner sees, hears, or feels your message and infers your thoughts, feelings, and desires. Your partner decodes your message to discover the meaning you want to share. Partners misunderstand each other when they are unaware of the different interpretation given the same word

---

EXPLORE 4.2A: Private Meetings

With your partner, take some time to consider several code words you currently use. Try to describe in detail what you mean when you use these words. Some possibilities may be: "listen up," "cool," "super," "nice," "stupid," or "ridiculous."

What other words could you use in place of these, if they were not available? Give examples of how your voice and body language affects the meanings of your words. Make it safe for your partner to free associate and link feelings to previous experiences, old wounds, hurts, or fears. For example, "When I hear or see this situation or word, I feel _____ , and it takes me back to this unpleasant situation _____. Now that I know these links, I would like to change in this way _____."

or gesture by the other person. Since you each give your own special definitions to key words and gestures, these differences may lead to arguments over who is "right." Neither partner can win this type of argument. To avoid these misunderstandings, it is important for the sender and receiver to use the same "code system."

When Difficulties Occur

When you and your partner have difficulty using the message restatement/confirmation steps, slow your conversation and patiently state each message fully. Allow for a complete restatement (feedback) by the listener and a confirmation of the listener's summary by the sender.

By going more slowly and by being sure to carry out each step, you often can locate the source of many problems that may arise in your communication process.

Conflicts and gridlocks between spouses usually reflect clashes and frustrations of their dreams. Use

Explore 4.2B to open yourselves to the hopes and dreams that underlie a conflict or problem. In these ways you reframe problems to become challenges and opportunities for growing in your love.

You have the ability to respond to persons in one of two ways: *"I value myself"* or
"I do not value myself."

You also have the ability to respond to your partner in a similar way:
"I value you as my spouse" or
"I do not value you as my spouse."

Practice Your Skills

At first you may feel clumsy or awkward when you explore details of your communication. This is normal, and with continuing practice you will become more comfortable with better ways to communicate with each other. Improving your skills takes a lot of effort and willingness to try. The brief suggestions in this book are not complete enough to enable you to make major changes in your patterns

---

EXPLORE 4.2B: Response Patterns

With your partner, consider how you each respond when you have disagreements. Listed here are words and phrases that describe possible ways to respond. Make a copy so you and your partner can answer independently.

Separately, put a check or X beside the eight words that best describe your own responses in times of disagreement between you and your partner. Answer as you see yourself.

She	He	Type of Response	She	He	Type of Response
____	____	1. withdraws	____	____	11. threatens
____	____	2. negotiates	____	____	12. pretends
____	____	3. gives in	____	____	13. looks openly at issues
____	____	4. forces own way	____	____	14. retreats, hides from issues
____	____	5. clarifies	____	____	15. begrudges, resentful
____	____	6. becomes silent	____	____	16. leaves room, vacates
____	____	7. blames someone	____	____	17. pressures, pushes
____	____	8. explains	____	____	18. surrenders
____	____	9. criticizes	____	____	19. disappears
____	____	10. evades the issue	____	____	20. compromises

After you have checked the eight responses you most typically make to a disagreement, transfer both sets of answers to Explore 4.2C on the next page. In that box put your initial beside the words you chose.

EXPLORE 4.2C: Response Patterns

As Seen From Viewpoint of Self

ATTITUDE TOWARD MY PARTNER

	I value and affirm you.	I do not value and affirm you.
I do not value and affirm myself.	DECLARE ["I messages"; I win and you win]	DEMAND ["you messages," fears; I win and you lose]
	2. negotiates 5. clarifies 8. explains 13. looks openly 20. compromises	4. forces 7. blames 9. criticizes 11. threatens 17. pressures
I value and affirm myself.	DEFER [too dependent; I lose and you win]	DEFECT [leaves partner; I lose and you lose]
	3. gives in 6. becomes silent 12. pretends 15. begrudges 18. surrenders	1. withdraws 10. evades 14. retreats 16. leaves room 19. disappears

ATTITUDE TOWARD MYSELF

of communication. Your support couple, pastor, or counselor has additional aids to help you practice your skills. They can tell you about marriage-relationship inventories that are available to assist you in looking at your personalities, expectations, and goals in several areas of your relationship.

Examine how your own style relates to the style your partner shows in this exercise. Your answers may cluster in more than one box. Discuss some examples of the way each of you shows your approach to disagreements. Which attitude and style do you each prefer? Talk about how you want to modify the ways you handle your conflicts.

A Serious, In-Depth Growth Challenge

For the next exercise allow an hour with a video (or audio) tape recorder and privacy. Tape record yourselves in brief (five minutes or so) conversations on any topic.

You may need a few brief practice trials so you can become more comfortable with the recording process. This can help you recover from the possible initial discomfort of hearing your own voices and observing yourselves on tape. After responding to the statements, you and your partner can compare answers.

When you complete the checklist, identify specific points at which you could have improved the taped conversation. Talk about your insights and feelings during this exercise. Rewind the tape to a specific place that was especially important in the conversation. Start with that response and then form more positive responses that can carry the conversation in a direction that you both prefer. Identify how you do this so you can do it again. Find ways to use your improved responses in other situations.

Give each other a big hug and tell each other that no matter how the taping went, you still love each other and want to learn more about ways to show your care to your spouse.

EXPLORE 4.2D: An In-Depth Opportunity

First, choose a topic you are willing to record. Then, tape a short (five to ten minutes) conversation. Short sound bites allow you to focus on your topic and have time to review, identify changes you want, and then tape again, like an instant replay of your conversation.

Next, replay the tape all the way through. Notice the way you use the elements of communication when you are the speaker (sender) and when you are the listener (receiver).

Use the following code:

     1 = not aware of this in my taped conversation
     2 = aware of this but did not do it at all
     3 = did this some but could have done it more
     4 = did this well, satisfactorily
     5 = did this very well, as often as needed

Rating of Speaker

Woman	Man	When Person Sent Messages
_____	_____	1. Sender was completely clear about message to be sent.
_____	_____	2. Sender checked with listener to be sure she or he was ready for message before sending it.
_____	_____	3. Sender used words that had same meaning for listener as for sender.
_____	_____	4. Sender stopped speaking occasionally to be sure listener was receiving accurate message.
_____	_____	5. Sender was open to feedback and encouraged listener to ask that message be repeated or clarified.
_____	_____	6. Sender easily distinguished between his or her message and the reactions of the listener to the message.

Rating of Listener

Woman	Man	When Person Received Messages
_____	_____	1. Listener encouraged sender by being willing to listen.
_____	_____	2. Listener turned and faced sending partner, looked at him or her.
_____	_____	3. Listener put other thoughts aside and gave full attention to sender and message.
_____	_____	4. Listener placed own reactions aside in order to become fully aware of partner's feelings and meanings.
_____	_____	5. Listener summarized message as feedback, so that sender could confirm accuracy of listener's understanding of message.
_____	_____	6. When message was unclear or too fast, listener stopped sender and asked him or her to repeat or clarify message.
_____	_____	7. When sender paused or was unable to find the exact word, listener waited patiently, speaking only if requested.
_____	_____	8. Listener helped sender be aware of listening levels by informing sender when he or she wanted to give feedback, send a reply, or continue to receive more messages.

4.3

CHALLENGES, FORGIVENESS

Forgive, and you will be forgiven; give, and it will be given to you . . . . For the measure you give will be the measure you get back.   *(Luke 6:37-38, NRSV)*

Define Problems as Challenges

Problems do not just happen. On the contrary, a situation occurs and in response to it you and your partner decide whether it is a problem or a challenge for either or both of you. Not all disagreements need to become problems. When you allow yourselves room to disagree and still to be accepted without losing face, many conflicts can be resolved quickly. As a couple you create your own marriage lifestyle, which includes disagreements, heated arguments, conflicts, and differences of opinion. These are opportunities to grow in love.

Conflicts, Crises

A conflict exists when you try to do two or more things but it is possible to do only one. Conflicts also arise when you do something that prevents your partner from doing what he or she wants to do. Disagreements become problems when you do not like what is happening but cannot reach a mutual compromise.

A crisis is that point at which things seem to be happening faster than you can respond with the resources you have. A high level of stress is one sign of a crisis. Typically, a crisis implies that several troublesome events have happened to you in a short span of time. In a sense, the additional problem in a crisis may be that you cannot cope with the problems you already seem to have. You can see a crisis as a disaster that will destroy you, or you can use a crisis as an opportunity to grow through learning new ways to deal with problems.

Steps in Problem Solving

An event becomes a problem when either or both of you desire to change the outcome in some way. To resolve a problem, you and your partner can take these basic steps.

1. Agree on Time, Place, and Topic to Discuss

Before you work on the problem itself, agree on the ground rules, or procedures, to guide your problem solving. Find a time that allows uninterrupted discussion of the issue, with only you and your partner present. It should not be when either of you is rushed or when something else requires your attention. Agree clearly on which problem you will consider, how long you will discuss it, whether anyone else should be present, and any other guidelines you feel necessary. A good problem-solving contract might be stated in this way: "We agree after dinner this evening we will decide which trip to make over the long weekend."

You also may agree that neither partner will mention the problem before the time you have set to discuss it.

2. Describe the Situation or Issue Clearly and in a Way That Is Agreeable to Both of You

To begin problem solving, be sure that both partners are discussing the same issue. Be specific, letting each partner reflect his or her understanding of the problem and its details. Start by describing the actual event in question.

To check yourselves, you might pretend you are taking pictures of the problem situation so all you can see is the behavior of each person involved. After the behaviors are clear, then allow more time to describe the interpretations, feelings, and intentions of each partner, in relation to the behavior. Be careful to state any inferences about your partner as being the way you see the situation, not as facts. Here are some contrasting statements:

Not this:
- You don't love me like you used to. (too general)
- You're not going to like this. (self-fulfilling prediction of failure)
- You don't want me to have any fun. (mind reading)

More helpful:
- When you yelled at me last night, I felt angry and frightened, because I thought you did not like me. (states specific time and behavior and your feeling about it)
- I would like to please you, but I feel so uncomfortable with your parents' criticism of us. (describes inner conflict about an invitation)

3. State the concrete, specific ways in which a situation or behavior creates a problem for you.

To the other person, that behavior may not seem to be a problem. For instance, if you do not like a certain type of clothes your partner wears, state the specific way this hurts you. It is not enough just to say, "I don't like it." It is essential that each of you state the way the behavior directly affects you.

Each of you has many behaviors. Some of these are a problem for you, but not for your partner; some may be a problem for your partner, but not for you; and some may be a problem for both. Sometimes the same behavior may present a different problem for each partner. Try to deal with one problem at a time. Don't be surprised if one clearly stated problem seems to lead to other problems. Acknowledge the other problems, but continue to work on the issue you agreed to discuss. Hold the other issues for other problem-solving sessions.

4. State Your Present Reactions to the Problem

In stating the problem clearly, you included your feelings, interpretations, and intentions. Usually, you also have some feelings about having the problem, in addition to whatever feelings you had in the original problem situation itself. In other words, the problem affects you now in some definite way.

In the illustration given in Step 2, the person may have felt "angry and frightened" as part of the original problem. In addition, that person now may feel guilty about having those feelings or may be hesitant to talk about the event. In the situation concerning contact with parents, the partner may want to maintain a good relationship with the relatives and yet avoid unpleasant criticism. These secondary feelings, which usually result from your sense of self-worth (your ego), can alert you to hidden investments you may have in the outcome of the problem. If you do not identify those investments clearly, you may choose a solution in order to prove you are right, rather than choosing one to solve the original problem. If you can determine your self-investment, you can consider it as you develop a solution. This enables you to focus upon the full range of needs that you each have as persons.

5. State Your Objectives Clearly

As you consider the problem, describe specific goals you want. Identify which person needs to make each change. Give your specific opinion about an outcome that would be better for you and for others involved. Compare these objectives.

Not this:
- I want things to be better. (not specific)
- You must never do that again. (a demand)

More helpful:
- I'd like for our lovemaking to be more relaxed, with more patience from you, at a slower pace. (specifies goal)
- I want us to be able to save at least five percent of our income this year. (states long-range goal)

Each partner needs an opportunity to state both the problem and the objectives as she or he sees the situation. These statements need to be clear enough so that each partner can easily state the other's perspective. You may not agree with your partner, but you can summarize what you hear him or her saying.

6. Consider Carefully All the Possible Alternate Solutions and Your Resources for Applying Them

After you agree on the problem, state your reactions to it, and agree on objectives; you can brainstorm possible solutions. In this step, don't worry about whether your ideas are practical or exactly right. It is usually helpful to take notes or to have some other way to keep up with possible answers. By developing several possible alternative actions, you can select the one that seems best, rather than taking the first one that comes to mind.

Together, evaluate your list of solutions in light of your goals and standards. You may use a values-clarification procedure, such as ranking your responses according to the way they fit your moral standards.

Your attitudes are important, and you and your partner are valuable resources, yourselves. Look for inner beauty and possibilities.

Sometimes you may need to seek new information or assistance from reliable sources. Either or both of you may ask for help from others and listen to their suggestions and insights, but you do not have to follow their advice or suggestions. However, in some areas involving others, such as money management, property, or employment, good information about what legally can be done, or about the possible results of alternate actions, can aid you greatly in choosing a solution. In deciding with whom to talk about alternatives, it is best to choose a trusted friend, mentor couple, minister, or professional person who is not directly involved in the problem in any way, since that will leave you and your partner free to make your own decisions.

7. Choose Your Plan and Carry It Out

In solving any problem, the time comes when you must act. You cannot choose not to choose, nor can you choose not to act. Even if you indefinitely postpone making changes, that is a choice; although it may be a solution with results that are worse than the problem.

You probably never will have all the information and resources you would like in order to find a guaranteed answer to your problem. Nevertheless, out of the possible solutions you and your partner have discussed, select one and actually implement it.

Your action plan may require changing the way you speak to your partner, rearranging your schedules, or taking a different view of the situation in order to make it less disturbing. It should give you as much control as possible over the outcome. The success of your plan will depend upon how well you and your partner carry it out.

8. Evaluate the Outcome of Your Actions

When you check the results of the action you took to resolve the problem, you will gain feedback about your new patterns. This is helpful for two reasons. First, you achieved the goal you set as a solution, and you will be able to reserve your plan as a possible strategy when a similar problem arises in the future. And second, if your action did not resolve the problem, then you could check to discover the reasons, return to Step 1 to reformulate the problem more precisely, and be better informed about the reason your action did not work.

Often a solution only partially achieves the objectives you set in Step 3. Look at the plan and the

---

EXPLORE 4.3A: Problem Solving and Feedback

With your partner, think about a recent conflict, disagreement, or crisis that was a problem for one or both of you. Use the seven steps we have listed to develop a plan. Then apply the plan to the problem. These seven questions reflect the seven steps:

1. Which problem do you agree to discuss, when, and where?
2. Have you clearly described specific behaviors, feelings, interpretations, and expectations that relate to the situation?
3. Have you each stated how the situation is a problem for each person involved?
4. What are your current reactions to the problems?
5. What objectives would you like to accomplish? Do you agree on these?
6. What alternate solutions have you outlined?
7. Which solution will you use? Who will do which parts? How? When?
8. What happened as a result of your action? What are the next steps you need or want to take? Encourage and embrace each other at times and describe your own feelings during the process.

results in detail so both of you can identify which actions helped and which were not effective in reaching your goals. Continue the effective actions and agree on additional problem-solving sessions to improve other parts of your original plan.

Your Reset Button

It would be great to have a reset button you could press to get out of any mess you find yourselves in and start over at the more positive place you were before the mess happened. The mess may be anger, harsh words, feeling forgotten or left out, resentment, or other hurts that have pushed you and your spouse apart. *Forgiveness is your reset button to restore your relationship when it is damaged.*

Marriage is about intimacy, and intimacy requires safety. Intimacy involves our private world of fears, needs, joys, and hopes that no one else gets to see. It is a great privilege and responsibility to be invited into these most private areas. Therefore intimacy is always fragile, vulnerable, dangerous, and needs to be handled with great care. Trust is not blind. We need information to decide whether to trust. So you each need to know for sure you will not be hurt when you open your most private self to your partner.

Trying to keep the upper hand by holding onto resentment keeps you from being intimate and deeply involved, but it also misses the fun of freely being yourselves and finding better ways to love, care, and grow. Instead of combat and manipulation, seek peace, sharing, caring.

Forgiveness and Reconciliation

What if you spend many years withholding yourself from your partner because of resentments about past events, all along thinking you are the victim. You can stop playing the victim and living in the past, because you are cheating both your partner and yourself. The reset button allows us to start afresh where we are. When we are willing to let go of old hurtful attitudes and relationships, we are open to our future. We have a new spirit and love of life.

Forgiveness is our reset button that enables us to start afresh and restore our positive relationships. To forgive is literally to give up resentment and no longer claim that the other person owes you something. You are reestablishing your relationship without asking for anything in return. You give without expect-

ing the other person to be perfect, which makes sense since we ourselves are not yet perfect either. In our God-given core being we have self-worth, dignity, and confidence.

Often we fall in love with what we hope our partner is, not with who our spouse really is. If we are afraid, we try to hurt the other person before that person can hurt us. But this is giving power to those who have hurt us in the past. Reset says, "I will take my power and energy and apply it to where we want to go, not to where I have been."

Steps to Reconciliation

What are your big goals, your big picture? What positives do you want from your marriage? Chances are your spouse also wants similar positives. Are the negatives worth giving up the positives you both want?

Next, ask what pattern are you in? How is your pattern working for you now? If not, reset by checking how you can make it safer for your partner to be close to you.

What changes can you make to make it safe for your partner? How can you provide a safe place for your partner to be open, accepted? Feeling safe allows one to be open. This is the grace of love. We don't need someone to tell us whether we are loved. We do need someone to show us it is safe to come closer in love.

Monitor the change. Ask for feedback. Observe whether your partner feels more secure and loved because you have changed in some specific way. Reset says, "I will not give into the fear. Instead, I will set a standard for care and go the course to win together." As you repeatedly replace hurtful patterns with positive caring actions, you create a new pattern that now becomes the norm for you. This takes a long time, yet continuing to practice your new care gradually convinces your partner your change is genuine, dependable, and permanent.

Openness and Respect

Throughout the problem-solving process, it is essential to respect each other's feelings and opinions and to accept honest differences in views. Some differences are expected in any relationship. A 100 percent agreement on everything in a marriage may be a sign that one partner is too dominant or the other is afraid to disagree. Seek to understand each other and to allow for individual views about facets of each problem.

The first time you use this problem-solving process, you may feel awkward or self-conscious. This is normal and to be expected. The procedure may seem mechanical or cold to some, but most couples who develop this type of problem-solving technique find that it works very well.

The results of this approach are well worth the investment of your time and energy. If you try to work through each problem when it is first noticed, you will prevent a buildup of the unresolved feelings and habits that lead to resentment and separation. In addition, successful problem solving builds love and increases your confidence in yourselves and in your relationship.

Selected Resources

Marriage and Family Ministry-related websites:

www.smartmarriages.com
Information about resources, professionals, programs, research, and media concerning marriage, parenting, and family concerns, by the Coalition for Marriage, Family and Couples Education.

www.Family-project@uchicago.edu
Information on marriage research, programs, policies, and conferences.

www.gbod.org/marriage and www.gbod.org/family
Visit these websites for lists of resource persons, schedules of upcoming training events and opportunities, annotated lists of additional resources, and other aids for using the GROWING LOVE IN CHRISTIAN MARRIAGE Couple's Manual and Pastor's Manual.

Organizations:

Association for Couples in Marriage Enrichment (A.C.M.E.)
800-634-8325, *www.marriageenrichment.org*

Marriage Encounter: United Methodist Engaged Encounter: United Methodist 800-795-LOVE.

Printed Resources:

Dunn, D., and Dunn, B. *Willing to Try Again: Steps toward Blending a Family*. Valley Forge, PA: Judson Press, 1993.

Everett, W. J. *Blessed Be the Bond: Christian Perspectives on Marriage and Family*. Lanham, MD: University Press of America, 1990.
A careful description of marriage as sacrament, vocation, covenant, and communion in relation to a theology of marriage.

Gottman, J. M. *Seven Principles for Making Marriage Work*. New York: Simon & Schuster, 1997.

Ives, J. P. *Couples Who Care*. Nashville, TN: Discipleship Resources, 1997. Real-life stories of couples who are coping well.

Penner, C. & Penner, J. *A Gift for All Ages: A Family Handbook on Sexuality*. Waco: Word Books, 1986.

For additional resources visit *www.cokesbury.org* or call 800-672-1789.

In this space enter additional references your pastor, mentor couple, or counselor may suggest.

W.1

YOUR CHRISTIAN WEDDING

There was a wedding in Cana of Galilee, and. . . Jesus and his disciples had also been invited to the wedding.
(John 2:1-2, NRSV)

A wedding is for a day; a marriage is for a lifetime. Whether simple or elaborate, your wedding service has special meanings for you and your partner. Since your wedding expresses what you believe about marriage, it is more than just a ceremony. Your wedding expresses your self-understandings and your love for each other in the context of God's love for you. Your wedding does not have a money-back guarantee. Neither does it have a provision for exchanging your spouse, in case he or she does not match your anticipations or you measure up to your dreams and expectations.

To Wed Is to Covenant

The root word *wed* means to make a covenant, promise, pledge, or vow. The now-seldom-used *troth* suggests faith, fidelity, and truth. Here are some special meanings that your wedding service may have for you:

- an intentional voluntary vow made by both partners to love and care for each other without reservations;
- a public notice that you are a married couple establishing your own household;
- an acknowledgment of God's grace and presence in support of your marriage covenant;
- a separation from childhood homes, parents, and other relatives, with your marriage covenant the primary relationship;
- a reminder of your preparation for marriage with your pastor and support couples, and all that you have learned from families, friends, and other sources.

Some areas have a "Community Marriage Policy" in which all pastors and churches agree to require basic marriage preparation of every couple seeking a wedding. THE GROWING LOVE IN CHRISTIAN MARRIAGE program can fulfill this requirement.

Together, you and your partner can decide how to use these suggestions.

Meanings of Your Wedding for Others

Your wedding also has meanings for those who are close to you. When you espouse each other as husband and wife, you put each other first before all others. Anyone who may try to compete for being first in your lives is asked instead to support your union and not try to destroy it.

Meetings With Your Pastor

Consulting with your pastor can provide perspectives on marriage, opportunity to explore any personal concerns you may have, and orientation to details of your wedding. Your pastor is trained to adapt these GROWING LOVE resources to your specific situation. Your pastor has arranged supporting couples, classes, and other resources to support your strengths, sensitize you to important issues, and encourage your growth.

In addition to your conversations with each other, we hope you will meet several times with your pastor. We use the term "minister," or "pastor," to refer to the professional person with whom you discuss your relationship. This may be the pastor or associate pastor of your church, a minister who specializes as a chaplain or pastoral counselor, or a marriage counselor or therapist.

In an initial get-acquainted meeting, arrange to use this guide and any other supplementary materials your minister may suggest. You can also consider in-depth topics you, your partner, and your minister and/or mentor couple may suggest.

Some of these discussions may be as a couple and others may be as individuals. To talk about topics in this guide, ask questions, and examine areas that may have been difficult for you.

If you are using this guide prior to your wedding, plan time when you as a couple and your minister can consider the meanings of the wedding service and your own covenant for your marriage.

If you use this book after your wedding, connect these meanings to your good memories, joys, and anniversary celebrations.

Wedding Details to Check

Your wedding service is both a religious service and a legal proceeding. The exact requirements for marriage vary among the states, so you and your partner should consult with your pastor and/or appropriate public official concerning the legalities in your state. Some couples may have other legal arrangements to update before the wedding date. These may relate to establishing certain property as legally separate, updates in wills or insurance policies, modifying child custody details, or other matters that may require the aid of an attorney.

Your Wedding Service

Through your wedding service you express your commitment to manifest God's love, grace, and forgiveness in your marriage. Consult with your pastor early enough for you to reserve a time and place for your wedding and opportunities to participate in individual, couple, and group times, as described in the "Introduction" to this guide. Some churches may also have mentor or sponsor couples who can give you additional insights and support. Pastors and/or mentor couples may lead marriage education courses, retreats, or church workshops for couples. In this process with your pastor arrange for your wedding service, rehearsal (if needed), and related matters. References to additional types of wedding services are available in the resources section of this guide. If you have not completed the questionnaires available as part of this guide, it will be helpful if you will do so. Some ministers or counselors may offer additional couple-relationship inventories as a part of your preparation for marriage. You may already have completed some of these matters with your pastor and/or mentor couple.

Your wedding is a worship service, with its focus upon you and your partner as you give your pledges to each other before God. This can be done well in any type of wedding, whether it is a very simple, informal service with only a few persons present or a large church wedding. Matters of music, ritual, and attendants will be decided by you and your partner in consultation with your officiating minister. He or she often can assist you as you work with relatives and others in arranging the details. You may want to examine other wedding services as you and your pastor plan details of your wedding service.

Customs, traditions, and the wishes of parents and others are important considerations. However, with your pastor, you may design your wedding service to express the meanings you want to share. Choose your service on these merits, whether it is a traditional service or an unusual one. Remember to consider the policies of your pastor and church in these arrangements.

EXPLORE W1: Your Wedding Service

The standard United Methodist service of Christian marriage begins on page 864 of *The United Methodist Hymnal*. Carefully examine each section, noting especially the emphases on one woman and one man joining in equal partnership before God. With your pastor you may select other wedding services to examine.

Independently, you each can write words or phrases that express what your wedding means to you; then you can compare notes. You also might locate pictures, cartoons, or other materials that will help you talk about your wedding.

After your wedding you may return to this exercise and review wedding pictures, surprises, and stories about your wedding.

Some persons believe a wedding signifies a loss of freedom; that it is a mere ceremony so you may show off to others; or it means the end of happy times. Some may assume the wedding ceremony, or the marriage license, entitles one to insult, mistreat, or abuse one's partner in the privacy of the home. Share any negative views of weddings and marriage that might bother you now.

YOUR CHRISTIAN WEDDING

Our Marriage Covenant

As husband and wife together,
we have explored the four themes of our marriage,
faith, hope, love, and power

Wife: _____   Husband: _____

I, _____, pledge to you, _____
                husband   wife

and

I, _____, pledge to you, _____
                  wife   husband

In the context of God's grace to us,
I reaffirm my promise to love and cherish you always.

As God loves me, so I love you.

I pledge to you my continuing love and support
as we live, pray, play, plan, and work together.

Enter your names and then affirm aloud your marriage covenant promise to each other.

W.2
WEDDING INFORMATION

This information is to be filled in by the couple together. Dates should be set in consultation with pastor. Arrange to make copies of this information so you both and your pastor will have the same information.

Woman's full name _____

Address _____

_____
Phone Work _____ Home _____
E-mail _____

Woman's Parents' Names _____

Address _____

_____

Dates for premarital conference with pastor
Man _____ Woman _____ Couple _____

Dates for premarital conferences with physician
Man_____ Woman _____

Physician's name(s)_____

Dates for premarital conferences with sponsor couples
Sponsor Couple(s)_____

Have you secured the marriage license?
Yes ____ No ____ If not, when? _____

Wedding Rehearsal   No ____ Yes ____
Date _____ Hour _____
Place _____

Rehearsal Dinner?   No ____ Yes ____
Date _____ Hour _____ Place _____

Wedding
Date _____ Hour_____ Place _____

Where will the reception be held?
Hour_____Place_____

Man's full name _____

Address _____

_____
Phone Work _____ Home _____
E-mail _____

Man's Parents' Names _____

Address _____

_____

Maid of Honor _____

Best Man _____

Bridesmaids _____

Ushers _____

Other attendants _____

Who presents the bride in marriage? _____

Will you use one ring or two rings? _____

Organist _____

Soloist _____

Florist _____

Photographer _____

Other wedding details _____

_____
Your address after the wedding _____

_____
Phone(s) _____
E-mail (s) _____